FROM
PETER THE GREAT
TO LENIN

FROM
PETER THE GREAT
TO LENIN

A History of the Russian Labour Movement
with Special Reference to
Trade Unionism

S. P. TURIN

Routledge
Taylor & Francis Group

LONDON AND NEW YORK

First published by
FRANK CASS AND COMPANY LIMITED
by arrangement with P. S. King & Son Ltd.

| First edition | 1935 |
| New impression | 1968 |

Published 2005 by Routledge
2 Park Square, Milton Park, Abingdon, Oxfordshire OX14 4RN
711 Third Avenue, New York, NY 10017

First issued in paperback 2014

Routledge is an imprint of the Taylor and Francis Group, an informa business

ISBN 13: 978-0-714-61364-2 (hbk)
ISBN 13: 978-0-415-76043-0 (pbk)

PREFACE

In writing this book my chief aim has been to present an account of the Russian Labour Movement, based mainly on original Russian sources. I should not have ventured on this dangerous ground if I had not been persuaded that the materials and documents here collected may be of some use in filling in the gap which exists on this subject in the literature of this country.

The Labour Movement in Russia differed greatly from those of the chief European countries from its inception up to its final stage, and it would be a mistake to apply to it the same measuring-rod which we are accustomed to use for the Labour Movement of this or any other country of Europe. On the other hand, the Revolution of 1917 created universal interest in the " soviets." Before that the existence of soviets was hardly known outside Russia, although the whole history of the Russian Labour Movement rests upon them.

The object of the book is, therefore, to investigate the main trends of the movement; to analyse the origins and nature of soviets; and to describe the scope and character of the Russian Labour organisation. The latter will be treated here with special reference to trade unionism, for the trade union problem has not received adequate treatment outside Russia, and indeed, even in Russia itself it has not been investigated sufficiently. The existence of a fair number of books in English on the Socialist Movement in Russia makes it hardly necessary for me to describe it fully here. I deal with it, therefore, as need arises, mainly in connection with its influence upon the labour organisation in Russia.

Finally, I attempt to throw some light on the question of how far the present *régime* in the U.S.S.R., with all its strength and weakness, is the natural outcome of the prolonged struggle for freedom and independence by the Russian people.

No one can be more aware than myself of the defects and shortcomings of the pages which follow. I feel, however, that the opportunity which I have had of handling documents and materials that have already disappeared, or are rapidly disappearing, and my participation in the trade union movement, which I was able to observe from the inside at a highly critical period in its history, imposed on me a moral obligation to preserve some permanent record of them.

I have supplemented the book by the addition of two articles. The first is a Report on Workers' Family Budgets in Soviet Russia, which I communicated to the International Labour Office of the League of Nations in 1929 ; the second is a lecture on Russian Consumers' Societies, delivered at the Summer School of the Co-operative Party at Cober Hill, near Scarborough, in 1927. The former may serve as a basis for a study of the standard of life of the Russian workman ; the latter describes, though necessarily only in outline, the development of the Co-operative Movement in Russia before the Revolution.

The bibliography of Russian sources printed at the end of the book will, I hope, be of some use for a further study of Russian problems, especially as in their more recent works the majority of Russian economists, historians and politicians omit references to the pre-revolutionary literature. I have resisted the temptation to utilise sources published in languages other than Russian, and have made only a few references to them. I have also abstained from quoting any material published in Russian outside Soviet Russia, soon after the Revolution of 1917, as such material must be regarded as a secondary, and not a primary source.

My indebtedness to Sir William Beveridge, Professor Harold Laski, Sir Bernard Pares and Professor Lionel Robbins is great. Without their encouragement I should have found it difficult to complete my investigation.

I need hardly say how much my studies of Russian trade unionism have been inspired and guided by the works of Mr. and Mrs. Sidney Webb on the history and organisation of trade unionism in Great Britain.

I am deeply grateful to Professor R. H. Tawney and Mr. C. M. Lloyd for all their suggestions and their invaluable criticism during my study. It is needless to say that I alone am responsible for any arguments and conclusions contained in this book.

I have also to thank many friends for their help and assistance of all kinds, and my wife for her unfailing comradeship throughout the whole period of my study and work.

I shall have realised my aim if my book should prove of some use to students of Russian problems, and helps to elucidate them.

S. P. T.

London, 1935.

TABLE OF CONTENTS

FROM PETER THE GREAT TO LENIN

CHAPTER I

FROM PETER THE GREAT TO PUGACHEV

The Inception of Industry in the sixteenth and seventeenth centuries —Peter the Great and his Reforms—State Factories—The Organisation of Labour : *artels* and *starostas*—The Rules of 1741—Insurrections and Riots of Workers—The Pugachev Insurrection—The Character of the Russian Labour Movement.

THE Russian Labour Movement is two hundred years old. The first signs of industrial development in Russia appeared in the sixteenth and seventeenth centuries ; but production was sporadic and primitive in character, and goods were manufactured not so much for the open market as for the use of the Crown ; and internal and foreign trade alike bore a handicraft character. The early part of the eighteenth century marks the beginning of industry on Western lines, when Peter the Great decided to copy European methods of production in Russia. It was at this time also that the first shoots of free labour began to push their way through the bondage by which the social and economic life of Russia was overlaid.

In order to understand the experiments of Peter the Great in the sphere of production, and his attempts to guarantee a sufficient labour supply for newly-created industries, we must bear in mind that Russia at that time was just beginning to recover from the evils of civil strife, of " the Time of Troubles," and that the regeneration of the economic life brought with it the revival of the old political *régime*. " The nobles definitely seated themselves in the place of the boyars ; and out of their midst arose the new feudal aristocracy that made possible the flowering of the ' new feudalism ' of the eighteenth century." *

In the growth of Russian boundaries and in the increase of foreign trade much greater possibilities of use and development opened for merchants' and commercial capital, which had begun to accumulate in Russia long before the accession of Peter the Great. All the reforms of Peter the Great actually grew out of political and economic conditions. Peter the Great did not create his industries out of nothing.† There were present " all the conditions requisite for the development of large-scale production : there was capital (though in part foreign) ; there was a domestic market ; there were working hands."‡ But Peter the Great did not realise that it was impossible to drive commercial capital into artificial channels and that Russia was not yet ready for industrial development on a large scale. It was beyond Peter the Great's power to force capitalism on Russia artificially. It came to Russia in the latter half of the nineteenth century as a consequence of the natural development of the economic forces of the country.

The methods employed by Peter the Great to

---

* " Boyar—free follower of a prince ; member of highest social and political class in Russia until Peter the Great established the ' Table of Ranks ' (1722), which made rank technically dependent on service position (as it had already become in fact)."   M. Pokrovsky, " A History of Russia."   London, 1930, p. 240.

† " There can be no doubt, that during the periods successively of Peter's grandfather, father, elder brother, and sister, those reforms had at least undergone a partial initiation, and more than one Western innovation had been borrowed." V. Klyuchevsky, " A History of Russia." London 1926, Vol. IV., p. 215.

‡ M. Pokrovsky, *op. cit.*, p. 283.

foster industry in Russia are well known ; they
included the enforcement of strict regulations, the
establishment of monopolies, and grants of bounties
to manufacturers. His government encouraged the
free import of machinery from abroad and fixed high
duties on imported manufactured goods ; it supplied
the owners of factories with capital, with machinery
and with skilled labour from abroad. Manufacturers
were exempted from payment of various State dues
and taxes ; entire villages, with their inhabitants,
were placed at the disposal of factory owners in order
to ensure an adequate supply of labour. State
factories were transferred to private owners, together
with the workers employed in them ; free artisans
were no longer allowed to move from the factories in
which they were employed to other parts of the
country ; vagrants, illegitimate children, dissolute
women and criminals were sent to the factories. This
practice of Peter the Great reminds us of the means
used to procure labour in other European countries,
as, for instance, in Austria under Maria Theresa, or
in England, when the Act of 1802 was necessary to
defend the parish children against exploitation in the
factories.*

But in spite of the stringent measures taken, the
problem of an adequate supply of labour still
remained unsolved, and in 1721 Peter the Great
issued a decree which empowered noblemen to employ
their peasants in factories, and which gave them, as
well as the merchant class, the right " to buy entire
villages together with their bondmen, on condition
that these shall for ever remain attached to the
factory for which they were bought," that is, factory

* I. M. Kulisher, " A History of Russian Industry and Labour,"
in the Archives of the History of Labour in Russia. Petrograd,
1921, Vol. I., p. 30.

owners were not allowed to sell their factories separately from the workers employed in them. Later, in 1736, this decree was supplemented by an Order which laid down that not only bondmen, but all workers and their families should remain in the factories for ever, including those free workers who had no owners.* These two enactments legalised forced labour in Russian industry, and " our factories became real workhouses where order was maintained by strict discipline and onerous punishment was the only incentive to work."†

All Russian factories and works during this period belonged to one of three categories. There were, in the first place, State or Crown works ; secondly, there were private works, later called *possessional*, with workers attached to them ; and, thirdly, private works belonging to noblemen (later called *votchini* or " private estate " works).‡ H. Storch, a German economist and tutor to Alexander I., gives the following description of the first two categories : " The work in Crown and private mines is done by crown ' master-workers,' by peasants attached to the mines and by free labourers. The class of ' master workers ' consists of crown peasants and of men destined for the army, but who have been detained

---

* A. Bykov, " Factory Legislation in Russia." St. Petersburg, 1909, pp. 129, 130 ; V. I. Semevsky, " The Peasants during the Reign of Catherine II." St. Petersburg, 1903, Vol. I., p. 458 ; A. Afanassiev, " The National Wealth during the Reign of Peter the Great," in the *Sovremennik*, 1847, Vol. IV., Pt. II., p. 19.

† M. Tugan-Baranovsky, " The Russian Factories in the Past and Present." St. Petersburg, 1898, p. 23. Professor J. Mavor, in his book on the " Economic History of Russia," accepts this view of the position of labour in the time of Peter the Great : " Russian factory industry in the eighteenth century was founded upon the same basis as the cultivation of the soil, namely upon bondage, and the factories became veritable workhouses " (p. 126).

‡ The majority of Russian industrial undertakings at that time were either mines or iron works.

for work in the mines. These, as well as their descendants, belong to the private and state mines to which they are attached and are kept at the expense of the Crown or of the owners of the mines. Their wages vary from 15 to 30 roubles per annum, according to their qualifications. The cost of food which is bought by them in the stores is deducted from their salaries. The discipline, wages and punishments . . . are almost entirely military. Promotion is the same as in the army ; they are tried by court-martial, and the members of administration of the mines attend the court, if necessary. . . . Peasants attached to factories perform all kinds of unskilled work, and their ambiguous position led to numerous abuses."* The work in private undertakings which belonged to noblemen was done by their bondmen. As a rule, they worked three days a week at the works and three days in their own fields ; and at first no wages were paid to them for work done for their owners.

The Government, having started State mines and factories, issued several regulations to control the conditions and hours of work in them. The Admiralty Regulation of 1722 was the first enactment of this kind : it fixed the hours of labour for State works only, but it was adopted as a general rule by the majority of works and factories, and was in force until 1853—over a century and a quarter ! The working day fixed by this Regulation was ten hours in the winter months and thirteen hours in the summer. The bell calling the people to work tolled one hour before sunrise in winter (September 10th to March 10th) and tolled again one hour after sunset to dismiss them ; the dinner hour was from 11 a.m. to

* H. Storch, " Tableau Historique et Statistique de l'Empire de Russie à la fin du XVIIIième siècle." Paris, 1801, Vol. II., p. 394.

noon. In summer the bell tolled at 4.30 a.m., and again at 7 p.m., except in June and July, when work continued until 8 p.m. ; the dinner interval in summer was longer than in winter, lasting from 11 a.m. till 12.30 p.m. in March and April, till 1.30 p.m. in June and July, and till 1 p.m. in August.*

This division of the calendar year into only two seasons led to unequal length of the working day in the different parts of the country. The Regulation was amended in 1843, when Russia was divided into three zones—Northern, Central and Southern—with four seasons instead of two. The working day was fixed at 12 hours in summer, 9 in spring and autumn, and 8 in winter. The average working day fixed by the Regulation of 1843 was 10½ hours, instead of the 11½ hours of 1722.

The number of working days was 250 in the year ; the remaining 115 days were Sundays, feast days and free days (from 20 to 30 per annum) ; the latter were set aside to enable peasants working in factories to till their own land.†

It is an important fact that the wage system at this stage of Russian industry was of a primitive character. " The workman, if he was a bondman, hardly ever received his wages in cash. . . . Notwithstanding the government rule that wages were to be paid to bonded workers, hardly anything was left to them after their taxes had been deducted from

---

* K. Pazhitnov, " The Hours of Work in the Mining Industry," in the *Archives*, Vol. II., p. 19.

† " In the mining areas of the Ural and Altai Mountains work was usually done in two shifts of twelve hours each with a dinner interval of one hour ; in some mines there were shifts of eight and sixteen hours alternatively." Ben Von Fr. Hermann, " The Siberian Works and Mines," 1797, p. 172, cited by K. Pazhitnov. *Ibid.*, p. 21.

their wages ; this was particularly the case when they were employed in private factories."*

The first decree regulating wages was issued by Peter the Great on January 13th, 1724, and fixed the following rates of pay for work done " by men and horses " in the mines : " ten kopeks per day in summer for a peasant and horse, and five kopeks per day for a peasant without a horse ; in winter, six and four kopeks respectively."† The decree applied to unskilled workers only ; the wages of skilled workers and of foreign workers were higher, and a special wage scale had been drawn up for foremen, journeymen, apprentices and unskilled labourers employed in the State works in the Ural province ; this scale, like the Regulation of 1722, was adopted as a standard by other works, and for more than a century was used as the basis of the regulation of wages in the country.‡

The payment of extremely low wages during the first half of the eighteenth century needs explanation, which lies in the fact that the money wages of bondmen did not play an important part in their budget, as they were mainly paid in kind ; that the cost of living in Russia at that time was very low ; and that the legal position of workers was such that neither owners nor Government saw any reason to trouble about their wages.

There was another factor affecting the workers' condition at that time : the system of factory stores. The establishment of these stores was dictated by

---

* A. Lappo-Danilevsky, " The Russian Trading and Industrial Companies in the First Half of the Eighteenth Century." 1899 (St. Petersburg), pp. 69–70.

† K. Pazhitnov, " Wages in the Mining Industry," in the *Archives*, Vol. III., p. 7. See also : J. Hessen, " A History of Miners in the U.S.S.R." Moscow, 1926, Vol. I., p. 52.

‡ K. Pazhitnov, in his " Wages in the Mining Industry " (*op. cit.*,

pure necessity ; the workers had to be supplied with food and other necessaries because factories, in the majority of cases, were built far from villages and trading centres, especially in Siberia and the Ural Mountains. " Supplies for the workers, according to the decree of the 11th February 1724, must be laid in for a whole year and money to pay for them must be deducted from wages or salaries."* Factory Rules issued in 1735 give details of the sale of provisions to workers at factory stores : " the quality must be good, weights and measures correct, and prices must not exceed cost price plus 10 to 20 per cent. to cover overhead charges."† But, notwithstanding this Regulation, the prices at the stores were very high, and this made the position of the workers unbearable. " Many workers, after deductions of payment for bread had been made from their wages, received from 1·25 to 3 kopeks per month. And buckwheat, meat and clothing had to be bought out of this balance."‡

The conditions of work in the newly-erected factories and works were also very unsatisfactory. A special Commission, appointed by the Government

Vol. III., p. 8) gives the following rates of wages paid in the State factories in the Ural province :—

		Roubles per annum.	
	1723	1737	1766
Foreman (foreign) .	100	36	36
Foreman (Russian) .	24–36	30–36	36
Journeyman . .	15–24	15–24	24
Apprentice . . ⎱	12–18	10–15	12–18
Unskilled Labourer ⎰			

This table indicates, in the first place, the reduction in the wages of foreign foremen, and, in the second, the amazing stability of rates of pay for unskilled labour ; nominal wages remained at practically the same level for nearly fifty years.

* K. Pazhitnov, *op. cit.*, Vol. III., p. 11.

† *Ibid.*, p. 11.   Compare also A. Lappo-Danilevsky, *op. cit.*, p. 69, etc.

‡ *Ibid.*, p. 12.   See also M. Tugan-Baranovsky, *op. cit.*, p. 25 ; V. Semevsky, *op. cit.*, Vol. I., p. 547.

to inquire into the position in these industries, reported that low productivity of labour and the bad quality of manufactured goods were due to " the very bad buildings in which work was being done ; the lighting was inadequate and the roofs leaked . . . in the majority of undertakings there were no covered floors . . . there were no stone, brick or wooden floors. . . . The workers were badly dressed and few of them had a whole shirt to their backs."* As a result of this inquiry two decrees were issued by the Government on September 2nd, 1741 ; one was called the Regulation, the other the Workers' Rules ; but neither of these found favour with the owners, who simply ignored them, and soon they were forgotten by the Government, which took no steps to enforce them.†

The low rates of wages, the rise in the cost of living and the unbearable working conditions led to riots of the Russian semi-servile peasants, engaged in the State and private enterprises. " The annals of history are full of slave insurrections and of semi-servile peasant revolts," say Sidney and Beatrice Webb in their " History of Trade Unionism." " These forms of the ' labour war ' fall outside our subject, not only because they in no case resulted in permanent associations, but because the ' strikers ' were not seeking to improve the conditions of a contract of service into which they voluntarily entered."‡ In Russia this type of insurrection of semi-servile peasants became to a certain extent the predecessor of the Russian Labour Movement, and

* M. Tugan-Baranovsky, *op. cit.*, p. 26 ; A. Lappo-Danilevsky, *op. cit.*, p. 83.
† A. Bykov, *op. cit.*, pp. 130–133. See also Appendix I., p. 177.
‡ Sidney and Beatrice Webb, " The History of Trade Unionism." London. Ed. 1919, p. 2.

on these revolts actually rests the history of the Russian labour organisation.

The most serious, persistent and characteristic revolts occurred in the famous metal works in Lipetsk, in the paper-mills owned by Count Sievers near St. Petersburg, and in the Demidov iron-works in the Urals.

The metal works in Lipetsk, to which 1,300 peasants were attached, had been handed over by the Government to Prince Repnin in 1754. The conditions of work immediately changed for the worse, and the management began to treat the workers as ordinary bonded peasants. The workers then decided to ask the Government to take them back into the State works. In their petition, which was put before the authorities by their representative, Kuprianov, they stated that their wages, which had been fixed by decree at from 4 to 5 kopeks a day, had been reduced to 2 and 3 kopeks, and piece work from 50 kopeks to 20·5 kopeks per pood ; that cash payment had been replaced by payment in kind : by ' scythes, knives, mittens, wax, incense and horses,' which were unsaleable owing to the high prices fixed for them by the management ; and that deductions of taxes from wages were introduced by the management, whereas they had already been paid to the noblemen, and workers were thus obliged to pay their taxes twice over. The right of the management to send undesirable workers to the recruiting offices further added to the workers' discontent, especially as the State workers were exempt from military service. The presentation of the petition did not pass unpunished, and a special detachment of soldiers was sent to the factory to flog Kuprianov before his assembled comrades ; the workers set upon the soldiery and liberated Kuprianov. After this, they decided to create their own management, called the *Stanichnaya Isba* or District Peasants' Court, of which Kuprianov was elected chairman. The *Isba* used to send its representatives with petitions to the Government and collected money for the upkeep of the organisation. Workers who refused to join the *Isba* and to obey its orders were severely punished : in one case a man was beaten ; in another, all the doors and windows of a worker's house were taken from their hinges ; the wife of a third was dragged from her house by her hair and beaten.*

Another characteristic struggle had taken place in a paper-mill which had been given over by the Government to Count Sievers in 1753 and was, after his death, sold to Lieutenant Khlebnikov. From 1753 until 1802 the workers struggled here continuously for the restitution of their rights as State workers. They resented the cruel system of corporal punishment practised in the factory and insisted that floggings must be carried out in the presence of witnesses, before an assembly of workers.†

The Demidov works in the Ural Mountains afford a glaring instance of the cruel treatment of workers. According to the figures collected by the workers themselves, and put before the Government, 328 workers had been flogged in two of the Demidov plants between the years 1757 and 1760, and one of the men so flogged had died of his injuries, while a number of others were maimed for life. When the workers in Nikita Demidov's works rebelled in 1760, 500 Cossacks, and dragoons with a gun, were sent to

* V. I. Semevsky, " The Peasants during the Reign of Catherine II.," Vol. I., p. 487, etc.

† The origin of this demand was evidently Peter the Great's decree of 1736, in which it was laid down that floggings might only be carried out in the presence of all the workers of a factory, or all the villagers.

quell the rebellion ; 300 workers were arrested and sent to prison and their organisation, the *Zemskaya Mirskaya Isba*, was disbanded by the Government.*

Riots and insurrections of workers were particularly numerous in the sixties and seventies of the eighteenth century and fed the stream of revolutionary movement which was led in the south-west of Russia by the Cossack Pugachev. Pugachev's insurrection (1773–75) is frequently described by Russian historians as a revolt of the Ural Cossacks against the Government measures depriving them of their independence and conscripting them into the regular army ; the movement was, according to them, supported by the numerous nomadic tribes of the Ural Mountains and by the religious sects which had been driven to protest against the innovations introduced by Peter the Great. The modern literature on Pugachev in the U.S.S.R. categorically denies this interpretation of the movement, and views Pugachev as a national hero, who led the masses of the Russian people against the Monarchy and Capitalists.

In all probability the ultimate causes of the Pugachev rising lay very much deeper. There is no doubt that it was, primarily, the protest of peasants and workers against the intolerable conditions of bondage and of exploitation by the factory owners. Almost three-quarters of Pugachev's supporters were recruited from the ranks of the factory workers in the Urals ; these men were already in constant conflict with factory owners and Government officials ; they had created their own organisations for self-defence, and had their own leaders. The Government itself was aware of the rioting in the factories, and Catherine the Great in her speech on her accession

* V. I. Semevsky, *op. cit.*, Vol. I., pp. 513, 523 ; Vol. II., p. 369.

to the throne said that " at present 150,000 monastery and votchini peasants and 49,000 factory peasants are in revolt."*

The Pugachev insurrection affected fifty-six works in the Ural Mountains, the majority of whose workers joined the movement. There were, however, works which were against it : the Utkinsky workers, for instance, fought fiercely against Pugachev's Bashkir bands, and both sides lost more than 1,000 men. The same happened with the Syssertsky works. The explanation of this different attitude towards the rising is to be found in the existence of two different categories of workers : those who depended entirely on the wages they received from the works, and those who were only attached to the works temporarily and whose main income was derived from land. The latter were not specially interested in preserving the works as a source of employment.†

The Pugachev rebellion appealed to the workers as an opportunity " to take revenge for all they had suffered and to rebel against a social order which had brought them nothing but oppression." They had lost all hope of improving their position by peaceful means or separate insurrections, and realised that their only chance lay in concerted action, under the leadership of Pugachev, who promised them freedom from bondage and from onerous work in the factories. " Noblemen will no longer exploit the peasants by making them do onerous work and pay heavy taxes, for all men will be free and independent," said Pugachev in his Manifesto.‡

* N. Dubrovin, " Pugachev and his Associates." St. Petersburg, 1884, Vol. I., p. 352.
† J. Hessen, " The History of Miners in the U.S.S.R." Moscow 1926, Vol. I., p. 134.
‡ V. I. Semevsky, *op. cit.*, Vol. II., p. 504. This Manifesto was written by the associates of Pugachev, as he himself was illiterate.

The outcome of Pugachev's rising is well known ; his army of 15,000 men was defeated by Government troops under General Michelson ; he himself fled across the Volga, but was taken prisoner by his own associates and handed over to the Government. He was brought to Moscow by General Suvorov and was executed there. A punitive expedition was sent to the towns on the banks of the Volga and the population was mercilessly slaughtered by Count Peter Panin's Regulars.

The rebellion was at an end, but its results were far-reaching. The Government had awakened to the fact that reforms in the social and economic life of Russia could no longer be delayed. It had been made to realise that the position of the workers in the factories was anomalous and unbearable. " The workers," wrote Colonel Mavrin to the Empress from Orenburg during the Pugachev rising, " are the prey of factory owners who are robbers and who think of nothing but their own gain ; they rob their peasants of all they possess, for workers are forced to leave their homes, and are sent four, and even seven, hundred versts away to work in factories."*. And " in 1779, Catherine, who had learned a lesson from the bitter experience of the Pugachev rising, issued a decree for the improvement of the condition of workers employed in the works in the mining area. The work which employers were entitled to demand from their workers was strictly specified, the hours of work in factories and fields were fixed, and wages for unskilled labour were doubled."†

Such were the beginnings of the Russian Labour

---

* N. Dubrovin, *op. cit.*, Vol. I., p. 356.

† K. Pazhitnov, *op. cit., Archives*, Vol. III., p. 7. See also H. Storch, *op. cit.*, Vol. II., Appendix, p. 48. "In summer a work-man with a horse was paid 20 kopeks a day, a worker without a horse 10 kopeks ; in winter 12 kopeks and 8 kopeks respectively."

movement. The *leitmotiv* of this movement was mainly a protest against unbearable working conditions, low wages, high prices at the factory stores, corrupt administration and corporal punishment, which included the use of handcuffs and of chains. The methods employed by the workers in their struggle were combination, petitions and delegations sent direct to the Tsar or Empress. There was a strong belief among the workers that " factory owners were afraid of no law on earth," and that only the Tsar or Empress could protect them from the cruelties of the management and of Government officials in the factories. When they failed to obtain a peaceful solution of their difficulties, the workers frequently came to the conclusion that the best thing they could do was to leave the factories *en masse*. This marks the second stage in the struggle, and can be compared to a strike ; the difference lies in the fact that the workers did not merely stay away from work, but left the factories for good and returned, together with their families, to their native villages, which were sometimes hundreds of miles away. Thus, for instance, the workers of the Demidov plants, aware that they were likely to be sent back to the works, issued the following warning to the Government : " If we are hunted down and forcibly sent to the factories, there will be bloodshed on both sides and we therefore warn you of this, and are sending this warning everywhere, so that we may not be held responsible for any bloodshed which may occur."*

It is very characteristic that while Russian industry still had the character of the mediæval crafts, and while the work was done mainly by bonded men, with the assistance of a few artisans

* V. I. Semevsky, *op. cit.*, Vol. II., p. 335.

attached to the factories for life, and by foreign specialists, the bonded peasants created, in times of acute conflict, their own organisations. These organisations did not last long, and either disappeared as the result of repression, or faded out as soon as the causes, which had brought them into existence, passed away. These spontaneous combinations, created in moments of struggle and revolt, naturally, did not bear any signs of guild organisation. There were, however, certain attempts, influenced apparently by the English and German workmen, to create permanent organisations for times of peace, built on the guild principle. The workers, for instance, in the woollen industry in Kazan, were, in 1724, already organised into *artels*, representing weavers, spinners, etc. The *artel* formed part of a community which was headed by a *starosta* (elder) ; the community elected judges, spokesmen, and other officials. The elected officers took an oath to serve the community truly and faithfully.* In some factories workers concluded collective agreements with the owners, and even offered to run the factory themselves on co-operative lines.†

* J. Possadsky, " The Workers' Fight for Freedom." 1876, p. 418, cited by Semevsky, *op. cit.*, Vol. I., p. 549.

† In 1802 the workers in Count Sievers' paper mills concluded an agreement with the management which is probably the first written agreement between workers and owners in Russia. According to this agreement the " master-workers " (skilled labourers and foremen) in the mills received, instead of a wage, as before, one-fifth of the selling price of the output, and each worker's family received 12 cubic yards of firewood a year. The lump sum of money received by the " master-workers " from the management was divided by them according to individual output and grade of work done. The nominal selling price of paper was fixed, by the management and " master-workers " in consultation, once a year in order to prevent fluctuations in wages during the course of the year ; prices were fixed after taking into consideration the actual price for which paper had been sold during the previous year. If the quality of the paper did not correspond to the requirements agreed upon, the " master workers " were obliged to take it back

The tendency to create permanent combinations of workers became more general in the later stages of the movement, when free labour appeared in the market. But at this early period the main features of the movement were the spontaneity of the labour organisation, a great belief in the triumph of justice, and the outbreak of revolts as the only means to attain the ends. " The real causes of peasants' revolts undoubtedly were the compulsory labour at distasteful work, the conditions under which that work was performed, the low scale of wages, and the uncertain arbitrary method of remuneration, for which the fiscal arrangements of the Treasury were much to blame."*

The workers' revolts in Russia seem to have proceeded in a reverse direction to those in England. In England " in the first place they mark," according to Professor R. H. Tawney, " the transition from the feudal revolts of the fifteenth century, based on the union of all classes in a locality against the central government, to those in which one class stands against another through the opposition of economic

for re-manufacture. A special clause was inserted in the agreement according to which, during temporary stoppage of work, the workers were to be paid at rates which were current at the mills before the agreement was concluded. A ten hours' working day was introduced in the mills by the workers, and women and children under 15 were no longer allowed to work in them. Later, the owners succeeded in lengthening the working day to twelve hours, and in lowering the age of children employed in the mills to 12 years. In 1814, when the relations between owners and workers became strained, the workers presented a petition to Alexander I., in which they asked that the factory should be handed over to them ; they intended to manage it themselves on co-operative lines, and were ready to pay the state 15 kopeks for each ream of paper produced. This proposal, which is interesting because it came from bonded men who had no legal status, was rejected by the Government. M. Tugan-Baranovsky, *op. cit.*, p. 138 ; V. Semevsky, *op. cit.*, Vol. I., p. 502.

* J. Mavor, " An Economic History of Russia." London, 1914, Vol. I., p. 466.

interests."* In Russia we find that the opposition of one class to another was the first stage of the movement, and the union of all classes against the central Government, the second stage.

* R. H. Tawney, "The Agrarian Problem in the Sixteenth Century." London. Ed. 1912, p. 322.

CHAPTER II

BEFORE THE EMANCIPATION

Russian Industry and Labour in the First Half of the Nineteenth Century—Wages—Labour Legislation—Strikes and Riots—Labour Organisations—The Influence of the *Decembrists'* Movement—The Economic Conditions of Russia on the Eve of the Emancipation.

RUSSIAN industry experienced great changes during the latter half of the eighteenth century. Hardly a tenth of the big works and factories established by Peter the Great survived. But new factories appeared instead, and their rapid growth was the best sign of the growing accumulation of commercial and industrial capital in Russia.*

This rapid growth of industrial enterprises was stimulated to a great extent by the increase of population and particularly of urban population.† But the main cause of this increase was the so-called *obrok* system, which actually created free labour in Russia long before bondage was formally abolished in 1861. The main outlines of this system were as follows. There were two classes of bonded peasants in Russia. The first consisted of those who were tied to the place of their birth and who had no right to move beyond the bounds of their owners' estates : they usually worked half of the week for their owners, and for themselves during the rest of the week. The

---

* When Catherine came to the throne in 1762, there were already 984 factories, and at the end of her reign the number had grown to 3,161. M. Tugan-Baranovsky, *op. cit.*, p. 42.

† According to the fiscal census of 1722, the population of Russia was 14 millions, of whom 328,000 lived in towns. In 1796 (the fifth fiscal census) the population had increased to 36 millions, of whom 1,301,000 lived in towns.

second consisted of peasants who, instead of working for their owners, paid them a fixed money tax (*obrok*) : this enabled them to leave their native villages and to look for work elsewhere, though they still remained bound to their owners.*

The employers themselves were in favour of the *obrok* system, as it gave them a chance of finding hands for their factories, and therefore it had been consistently encouraged by the Government since 1736 ; in 1762 owners were again reminded by the Government of the advisability of employing so-called " free-hired " men, and requested to " conclude contracts with them." The " free-hired " men referred to in the decree were, in the majority of cases, peasants who were paying *obrok*.† The owners took the fullest advantage of the decree of 1762, and soon one-third of all the workers employed in Russian factories became hired men. In 1769 hired labourers constituted 40 per cent, of the total number of industrial workers. The percentage of hired labour in the wool industry was 43, in the silk industry 53·3. In towns the ratio was even higher, and in the factories of St. Petersburg the percentage of hired labourers to the total number of workers was 67·6.‡

This explains why serfdom was abolished in Russia only in 1861. The institution of serfdom was " an envelope, and the actual solutions which existed within that envelope were extremely varied. In

---

* The average amount of *obrok* payable per head was from 1 to 2 roubles per annum in 1760 ; from 2 to 3 roubles in 1770 ; about 4 roubles in 1780, and 5 roubles at the end of the eighteenth century.

† The following laws and decrees on this subject were issued by the Government :—
> The Decrees of the Senate in 1752, of Peter III. in 1762, and of Catherine II. in 1762 ; Law of Alexander I. of 1816, and the Laws of 1824, 1835 and 1840.

(*Cf.* A. Bykov, *op. cit.*, p. 140 ; N. Rozhkov, "Town and Village in Russian History," Moscow, 1904, p. 74.)

‡ V. Semevsky, *op. cit.*, p. 606.

particular in so far as the serfs drew the greater, or a considerable part of their income from industrial or commercial pursuits, serfdom meant for the peasant population chiefly dependence of a financial character, the obligation to pay sums of money or taxes to the landowners. A peasant in such cases paid the *obrok,* as this money-tax was called, but beyond that was free to do as he pleased. This is why there existed in Russia, long before the abolition of serfdom, a class of persons free to dispose of their labour, although socially, and in the eyes of the law, slaves. The peasants, without ceasing to be serfs, not only built up the elements of a free working-class, but created from amongst their own ranks the elements of a commercial and industrial bourgeoisie."*

The appearance of hired labour in the market created great disproportion in the rates of wages of the Russian workmen. According to a Government Enquiry Commission of 1834, hired workers were getting twice as much in wages as " possessional " workers.† This naturally caused great dissatisfaction among " possessional " workers, who constantly clamoured for equal pay. This claim was pressed as generally as that of the workers in the eighteenth century to be returned to the State factories. There was even a project put forward in the 'forties of the nineteenth century by Prince Golitsyn, whom the Russian economists compare with Lord Ashley (Earl of Shaftesbury), to equalise wages of hired and " possessional " workers. His idea was not realised, but the Government was pressed to define more clearly the new category of

---

* Peter Struve, " Past and Present of Russian Economics " in the "Russian Realities and Problems." Cambridge, 1917, p. 58.
    † M. Tugan-Baranovsky, " The Russian Factory in the Past and Present." Moscow. Ed. 1922, p. 152.

labourers and to codify the various decrees and laws. One of the motives for this was the fear that the hired labourer might raise his head and turn one day against his master, and even against the Government itself, as soon as the seeds of free-thought, dropped by the Decembrists' movement in 1825, reached the factories and the peasantry. And such a codification was made in 1857, which was called " The Rules of Employment of Persons freely-hired."*

The general impression of these Rules is that men were treated not as citizens and human beings, but rather as domestic animals who must be looked after in order to ensure the productivity of their labour. The Rules did not improve the position of the workers, and no wonder, therefore, that they protested against onerous conditions of work, and that there were many serious conflicts with factory owners.

These conflicts show that a new stage in the workmen's organisation had been reached. Instead of sporadic attempts at combination in the *Isba*, which took its origin from the village meeting, there now arose several secret organisations, which could not be tracked down by the factory-owners and the police. The delegates and petitioners, who had formerly represented the peasants before the Tsar and the Government institutions, were gradually replaced by the *starostas* and *starshinas*, who became actual representatives and spokesmen during strikes and riots. The *starostas*, or monitors, were not mentioned in the Russian Law Code, but in peaceful times the factory owners even encouraged their election, as they helped them to settle outstanding differences between the workers and the factory administration.

* For contents of the Rules, see Appendix III., p. 182.

During a strike, however, they were considered instigators (*zachinshchiki*) and agitators, and as such were always punished more severely than the other strikers.

The peasants, working in the factories, had a high respect for the *starostas*, and were always ready to stand by them. As far back as 1820 we find evidence of a stubborn struggle for their recognition, when, for instance, the textile workers in Fryanovo, near Moscow, succeeded in introducing into the factory rules an article authorising them to choose *starostas* for the purpose of keeping a check on the payment of wages and supervising the issue of raw materials to the operatives.*

But we must not be tempted to consider the institution of *starostas* as the embryo of professional labour organisation. The workmen themselves regarded their *starostas* as their spokesmen, just as they regarded the elders in the village meetings. The appearance of the more constant, comparatively permanent representation of workers by *starostas* meant progress. But it was a step not so much towards the creation of separate professional organisations, like trade unions, as towards the consolidation of the idea of one general organisation of all workers.

Data concerning strikes in Russia during the period under review were very scarce. It was only after the February Revolution of 1917 that the mysterious veil covering information about the labour movement in Russia was lifted, and the Archives of the " Third Department of His Majesty's Chancellery " became available. The following conflicts, recorded therein, throw a new light on the

* V. Svyatlovsky, " The Trade Union Movement in Russia." St. Petersburg, 1907, p. 6.

character and nature of the labour movement in Russia before the Emancipation.*

In 1824 the workers of the " possessional " iron-foundry of Baron Henicke in the Ryazan province complained that the factory administration had reduced wages and prohibited the free use of wood and bricks from the factory estate for the building of their houses. As the workers received no satisfactory answer from the administration, they ceased work, and gathered in crowds in front of the " Zemsky Court." The police, with the help of a military detachment, sent them back to the factory, and two workers who showed resistance were arrested. This did not, however, stop the trouble, and in 1825 fifteen more workers were arrested for " permanent disobedience," several received corporal punishment and Baron Henicke was authorised to send any disobedient workmen to the recruiting office. He promptly sent four, who, however, did not arrive at their destination : on their way they were rescued from the military guard by their fellow-workmen and were never traced. Long before this the workmen had warned the Governor of the Province that they would not obey Baron Henicke's orders, as they considered themselves attached to the factory, but not to its owner, and therefore they held that he had no right to send them to the recruiting office.

The Military Court, which investigated the case, found several workers guilty, and these, after receiving severe corporal punishment, were sent to Siberia. The Governor of the Province stated in his report that the workmen had a secret agreement

* This Department, which corresponded to the modern " Cheka," or G.P.U., was formed by the Imperial Government soon after the Decembrists' movement of 1825, when it was realised that there was danger of revolutionary ideas penetrating to the masses of peasants and workmen.

among themselves, and had taken an oath to resist any Government orders which authorised the owners of factories to send workmen to the recruiting office, and to stand by each other, even if force and corporal punishment were applied to them.

In 1829 the workers of the " possessional " factory of Countess Belosel'skaya in the Orenburg Province declared a strike, and on behalf of more than 2,500 workmen, presented a petition signed by 1,200 of them. In this they insisted on the removal from the factory of the *ispravnik* (captain of the police), Heferling, and the release of their representative, Tarakanov, who was under arrest. The workmen, according to the Report sent by the Vice-Governor of Orenburg, were acting systematically, and had their own secret organisation : they forced the *ispravnik* to leave the factory, did not obey the instructions of the administration, collected money secretly among the villagers for their organisation, made a habit of leaving the works and the village without permission, behaved very independently, seized some of the officials, and released those workmen who had been arrested by the factory administration, drove the shop steward and his assistant out of the factory, dismissed a foreman and beat him, compelled their fellow-villagers to conspire with them, detained a courier with official reports on him, and induced the *ispravnik* to read the reports to them.

The Vice-Governor of the Province, after the arrival of an auxiliary military force, ordered all the workers to be called together in front of the factory. The soldiers surrounded the crowd, and the workers were asked to confess to all their offences : some of them did so, but the remaining 1,100 workmen continued to offer stubborn resistance. Corporal punishment was then applied to those who held out ; meantime, a priest, reading the Bible, appealed to the crowd not to resist any longer.*

In 1831 the inhabitants of several villages were ordered to start work in the Kolyvano-Voskressensky factory in the Altai Mountains. The peasants refused to do so, saying that they were not obliged to work there. After the " instigators " had been arrested, some of the villagers agreed to work in the factory, but the peasants of the village of Varukhino, near Tomsk, resisted vigorously, and soon this village became the centre of the movement. The peasants here not only refused to work, but even refused to choose new representatives to take the place of those arrested ; instead, they sent their own delegates all over the neighbourhood to induce other villages to

---

* The real causes of the trouble in this factory, as enumerated in the workers' petition, were—

1. Very low wages in comparison with those of neighbouring factories, and unnecessarily high deductions from wages made by the administration to cover the workmen's indebtedness for goods received from the factory provision store, and for other payments made to them in advance.

2. The very high price for bread fixed by the factory administration : 70 kopeks per pood, instead of the market price of 40 to 50 kopeks per pood.

3. Delay and irregularity in the payment of wages, and very unsatisfactory and chaotic settlement of workers' indebtedness to the factory.

4. Too heavy work, especially in cutting trees and preparing firewood.

5. Employment of old workmen in the works, which was bad for their health.

6. The requisition of horses belonging to the workmen for a much lower price than that at which they had been sold by the factory administration to the workmen two or three years before.

7. Employment of the factory workers for additional work such as road-making and repairing.

In addition to the above petition, the workers made an oral statement, according to which there were children under 12 working in the mines who were expected to reach a daily output of 150 poods of ore. If their output did not reach this figure, even by one pood or by one carriage of ore, they were deprived of their whole wage for the day.

join them. Military police then arrested 200 peasants in Varukhino. Next day a crowd of peasants from neighbouring villages appeared in Varukhino and insisted that the arrested men should be set free ; otherwise they themselves wished to be arrested. The same thing happened on the following day. Military police then surrounded the workers, and a priest was called for, but his attempt at persuasion was energetically rejected by the crowd. After that the Cossacks proceeded to inflict corporal punishment on some of the disobedient peasants ; the resistance of the crowd was broken and the men were sent back to their villages. The Cossacks then went on to deal with the 200 who were imprisoned in a barn, but as soon as the doors were opened, and twenty-five of the arrested men were asked to come out and give evidence, the whole 200 rushed at the Cossacks, shouting : " Do not give in, anybody ! hold firm ! " A struggle ensued which ended in the defeat of the workmen, and all those arrested after the fight were executed.*

Mention should be made here of the famous Nicholas Railway, connecting Moscow and Petersburg by a straight line. All the sorrows and sufferings of the Russian peasant are focussed here. For a whole decade many thousands of peasants were forced to work at its construction with nothing but their hands and a few primitive tools, as they stood up to the waist in the marshes. As a rule they were not only paid low wages, but often had to wait months for their pay. Strikes were dealt with by military force and corporal punishment ; the workers were only kept quiet by *vodka*, which was freely sold on the spot, and the sale of which was encouraged by

* K. Pazhitnov, " Strikes and Riots of the Factory Workers," in the *Archives*, Vol. I., pp. 86–90 ; and Vol. II., pp. 132–137.

the authorities, as it brought good profit to the State revenue.*

N. A. Nekrasov was not exaggerating the facts when he wrote his famous poem, "The Railway," in 1865. Here is one poignant stanza :

" The road is straight ; its banks are narrow ;
  Rails there are, and posts and bridges . . .
  And Russian bones line that road.
  Do you know how many there are of them, Vanya ?
      We laboured in the heat and in the cold,
      Our backs were eternally bent,
      We lived in dug-outs, we starved and froze,
      Were soaked in rain and died of scurvy . . .
  The foreman robbed us, officials flogged us,
      Poverty crushed us.
  We suffered all,
  We, who are the warriors of God
  And the peace-loving children of toil." †

The dominating theme of the labour movement at that time may still be described in the words already used on page 15, in reference to that of the late eighteenth century: "a protest against unbearable conditions of work, low wages, high prices, corrupt administration and corporal punishment." But a marked difference was beginning to appear in the psychology of the masses and their attitude towards the employers and the administration. After bitter experience in the past, the workers realised that their belief in the triumph of justice was an illusion, and that it was not enough to draw the attention of the authorities to the existence of wrongs. They became aware of the importance of having their own organisa-

* D. Kargin, " Labour on the Nicholas Railway," in the *Archives*, Vol. III., p. 120. See also V. V. Salov, " First Railways in Russia, 1836–1855," in *The Viestnik Evropy*, 1899.
 † Translated by L. T. from N. A. Nekrasov, " Verses." St. Petersburg, 1919, Vol. II., p. 87.

tions. The element of conspiracy entered into their still temporary and spontaneous combinations, and the idea of acting together not only in a factory, but in a locality, gained more and more ground.*

Even the revolutionary ideas of the Decembrists reached the factory workers, and in 1836 a secret political organisation was " discovered " among the pupils of the mining school at the factory of Messrs. Lazarev in the Province of Perm. It issued an appeal, in the course of which it stated :

" There is no law in any country of the world that permits the citizens of a state to own other citizens. But with us in Russia, the noblemen and those who possess capital have received from the Russian Emperors an unlimited right to have bondmen."

The appeal went on to describe the intolerable conditions of life of the lower classes of the population, and their sufferings. It denied the common belief that the Bible sanctioned the existing order. " The people of civilised countries fought against serfdom and became free citizens. In Russia, on the contrary, the yoke of oppression is growing, and in future, we presume, it will be even worse. Experience has shown that the greatness of a state depends upon the freedom of its citizens. But in Russia the yoke of serfdom remains, so the country will never attain to greatness. The foundation of a Society which will unite all citizens sharing the above views and which will endeavour to take the power out of the hands of those who unjustly possess it and introduce freedom, is the only salvation for Russia and its future generations. Noble citizens ! Let us for

---

* In Appendix II., p. 178, we give some information as to the growth of industry, wages and prices at the beginning of the nineteenth century.

the sake of this abolish serfdom, introduce freedom and thus earn the gratitude of posterity."*

The economic conditions of Russia clearly indicated also that bondage was not in great favour amongst the gentry. The growth of commercial and industrial capital had drawn the Russian gentry from a purely agricultural standing to trade and industry. In this transitional period Russia actually entered upon the path of capitalistic development and required a larger supply of free labour and capital. At the same time domestic discontent in the country was very acute, disturbances, peasant risings, strikes and riots among workers had become a permanent feature, and the Decembrists' movement showed the possibilities of an extension of the revolutionary movement. Alexander II. himself knew that it was hardly possible to postpone reforms, and his famous words : " It is better to abolish serfdom from above than to wait until it begins to abolish itself from below," sounded more like fear than the genuine love of a sovereign for his people.†

On February 19th, 1861, serfs were emancipated in Russia, and at that point the Russian labour movement entered upon a new stage.

---

* The author of this appeal, Peter Ponossov, and twelve of his associates, were severely punished : they were sent to serve in the Finnish and Caucasian armies. An enquiry, which was conducted on the spot by the Governor and the police, did not disclose any influence of the proposed Society on the local population, but the " Government was frightened by the incident, as it was the first case in which the protest of workers was based, not on economic grounds, but on ' wrong ideas '." As a result of this Count Speransky was instructed to form a Committee, to include two Ministers (of Education and Home Affairs) for the reconsideration of school curricula and the rules of admittance of bondsmen. (*Archives*, *op. cit.*, Vol. II., p. 133.)

† Bernard Pares, " A History of Russia." London.   Ed. 1926, p. 346 ; James Mavor, *op. cit.*, Vol. I., p. 376 ; M. Pokrovsky, " Brief History of Russia." London, 1933, Vol. I., p. 217.

CHAPTER III

AFTER THE EMANCIPATION

The Effects of the Emancipation—Conditions of Work in the
Factories—Factory Inspectors' Reports—The Institution of *starostas*
—Strikes—The Morosov Strike—The Act of 1886—The Socialist and
Revolutionary Movement in Russia.

THE effects of the Emancipation of 1861 on the
industrial system, hitherto run on forced labour, were
far-reaching. Every branch of industry was affected
by the Act of February 19th, 1861. The majority of
factories became deserted ; the peasants attached to
them left *en masse*. The Government mines and iron
foundries in the Ural Province lost 75 per cent. of
their workers, and these could not be replaced, even
at a very high wage. The woollen and cotton
industries experienced the same difficulties ;
the silk industry, which employed more skilled
labour, the so-called " freely-hired persons," was
probably the only one that did not suffer quite so
much.

Emancipation did not affect the conditions of work
in the factories to any great extent, for the Reform
was mainly concerned with the peasantry, their land
tenure and their personal liberties. The conditions
of life of the workers were of little interest to anyone
in authority. A book by N. Flerovsky on Labour
in Russia, published in 1869, described the life of
workers in such dark colours that later on, in the
'nineties, when the reaction was growing more
intense, it was withdrawn from sale and from use in
public as well as private libraries. N. Flerovsky

visited all the big industrial centres of Russia and came to the conclusion that starvation was general among the workers. " If a worker," he wrote, " begins to explain his deplorable position in public, he is declared to be a *podstrekatel*, or instigator of a riot, and punishment by flogging follows without mercy."*

After the Emancipation employers continued to include in their contracts with the workers conditions which would have seemed too onerous even in pre-reform times. Contracts with workers at that time were considered to be a private affair between employer and employed. Nobody paid any attention to the few regulations for improvements which had been embodied in the Government Act of 1857 ; they had actually been swept away by the Reform and had not yet been replaced by new ones All the recommendations of various Government Commissions (of 1871, 1873 and 1875) concerning child labour, the employment of women, night work and the protection of the health and life of the workers were disregarded.

The factory inspectors' reports, and especially that of Professor Yanzhul, revealed an appalling state of affairs in the factories.† Professor Yanzhul in 1882–83 inspected 158 factories employing 84,606

---

* N. Flerovsky, " The Working Class in Russia." St. Petersburg, 1869, p. 285. It is somewhat surprising to find that N. Flerovsky was not an enthusiastic advocate of factory legislation. On the contrary, his sympathies lay in quite different directions. " The only escape for Russia," said he, " from pauperism and misery, caused by capitalism, lies in the immediate transfer of all mines and factories to the factory *artels*. The *artels* would run production on co-operative lines, and would in this way make the existence of an individual *entrepreneur* quite superfluous. (Cited by K. Pazhitnov, in " Labour Conditions in Russia." St. Petersburg, 1906, p. 11.)

† Factory inspectors were first appointed in 1882.

workmen.* The average working day was 12 hours, but there were 34 factories where a 13 to 14 hours' day was worked, 3 with 14 to 15 hours, 4 with 16 hours, and some even had a working day of 18 hours. Written contracts existed only in a few factories : in most cases there were only verbal agreements. Pay-books hardly existed, and where they did, they varied in type and contents. In some there were inscribed very old regulations, which had been abolished long ago. In many cases, factory rules had merely received the sanction of the local police. Fines were very carefully enumerated in the books, and the following are some that Professor Yanzhul quoted :

For singing songs after 9.30 p.m., in the factory or in places not allocated for that purpose by the owner ; for bringing tea, sugar or other provisions into the workshop ; for washing underclothing in the common bedrooms ; for having a wash under the pump in the court of the factory ; for writing on the walls ; for wandering from one workshop to another ; for singing songs during work hours ; for visiting the common bedrooms of married workmen (this applied to bachelors only) or women's apartments ; children were fined 3 roubles (first offence) for fighting in the courtyard of the factory.

All these fines were entirely improvised by the

* The majority of these factories were cotton mills, where 9·6 per cent. of all workers were children under 15 years of age (8,112 children) ; 1 per cent. were children under 10 years of age, and 32·4 per cent. were girls. In some factories, like the Ramenskaya Manufacture, near Moscow, the number of children was very high : 438 out of 1,618 workers, or 26·3 per cent. Their average working day was twelve hours. Children were obliged to work on Sundays, and in several factories they were even fined if they refused to do so. Seventy-five per cent. of the children did not go to school at all. Factory owners did not care much about their education, and the Government's recommendation that schools should be established at the factories was considered by the majority of employers as an unnecessary extravagance.

factory administration : the existing labour regulations sanctioned the imposition of fines only in cases of absence from work or damage done to the owners' property. " The owner of a factory is an absolute sovereign ; he is not tied by any law, and often applies and interprets existing legal regulations at his own discretion. The workers must obey him implicitly ; if they declare a strike, he charges them 10 roubles apiece ; if they leave the factory grounds he fines them 1 rouble each. No complaints about fines can be lodged with a magistrate." According to the rules printed in the pay-book, the owner has complete control of the fines collected. In some factories they reached a sum of several thousand roubles.*

The method of payment of wages was also very unsatisfactory. Professor Yanzhul found that only in seventy-one factories did there exist any system of regular payment of wages : in the remaining 110, wages were paid at irregular intervals, usually two or three times a year, or at the termination of the contracts. It was quite natural, therefore, that the majority of workmen were in debt to the owners and to the factory provision stores. The latter usually kept the prices of commodities from 20 to 80 per cent. above the market rate.†

* I. I. Yanzhul, "Labour Conditions in Moscow Province." Report for 1882–83. St. Petersburg, 1884, p. 83, etc.

† Professor Yanzhul made a very interesting comparison of wages in Russia, United States of America, and Great Britain, according to which " American workers' wages were from 100 to 400 per cent. higher than in Russia. Women's wages in the textile industry in the United States of America were 300 per cent. higher than in Russia. In England, according to the investigations of Edward Young and G. P. Bevan, men's wages were from 50 to 400 per cent., and women's from 150 to 250 per cent., higher than in Russia." It is true, says Professor Yanzhul, that the Russian worker in most factories lived rent free, but this difference was not very significant, and amounted only to about 1 to 2 roubles per month. *Ibid.*, p. 115.

The reports of other factory inspectors did not differ much from that of Professor Yanzhul. The Chief Factory Inspector, J. Mikhailovsky, summarising the individual reports of inspectors, says : " The sanitary conditions in all Russian factories are extremely bad. There are no protective measures against extreme temperatures in the workshops, against dust, dampness, steam or poisonous gases— there is hardly any ventilation at all. The very high percentage of accidents, especially among children, is due to the absence of protective installations round the machines, although the owners of factories assert that the reason for accidents is the negligence of the workmen and children themselves. Severe cases of accident do not receive any special treatment at all.* Workers' lodgings provided by the factory administration were in the majority of cases quite intolerable. ' Married women and men, bachelors, children and young girls were all sleeping together in the same room.' ' Bugs and fleas are so numerous in the barracks that all the workmen prefer to sleep in summer out of doors '."†

To those suffering from such conditions of life and work, strikes appeared to be the only means of protest and defence. And strikes occurred during the two first decades after the Emancipation in nearly every district, and affected not only big industry, but home industry and such occupations as that of the *izvozchiki*, or cab-drivers. The first

* K. Pazhitnov, " Labour Conditions in Russia." St. Petersburg, 1906, p. 57. There was no question of any compensation for accidents, which, by the way, occurred chiefly among the children (45 to 67 per cent. of the total number of accidents). The administration usually tried not to register accidents, and one of the factory owners confessed to Professor Yanzhul that generally only those accidents were notified to the police which could not be kept secret. I. I. Yanzhul, *op. cit.*, p. 127.)

† K. Pazhitnov, *op. cit.*, pp. 47–55.

revolutionary " underground " labour organisations were also created at this time. The South Russian Labour Union was founded in 1874 and the North Russian Labour Union in 1878. They followed a programme similar to that of the First International, and succeeded in rallying round them the Russian revolutionaries and several hundreds of workers in the South and North of Russia, who became the main channels for the distribution of revolutionary pamphlets, journals and leaflets printed in Geneva or secretly in Russia itself.*

Some of the strikes were typical of the whole struggle, and they are known in the social history of Russia as landmarks of the Labour Movement. Such were, for example, the strike in the Krenholm cotton-mill near Narva in 1872 ; the strike in the St. Petersburg New cotton-mill in 1879 ; and the famous Morosov strike at Orekhovo-Zuevo in 1885.

The Krenholm Manufacturing Company of Narva employed 6,000 workers ; the conditions of work there were onerous and the workmen suffered greatly from the imposition of exorbitant fines and long hours of work. Rates of wages were low, but they suffered most from the internal police, attached to the mill since 1857, and composed of the *starostas* (foremen), nominally elected by the workmen, but actually appointed by the administration of the company. This internal police, constituted into a court, had the right of imposing fines equal to one up to ten days' wages ; of applying corporal punishment (from one up to fifty strokes) ; and of arresting workmen. It also had authority to deal with certain cases usually

* The programme of the North Russian Labour Union is given in " Economic Development and the Class War in Russia in the Nineteenth and Twentieth Centuries." Leningrad, 1924, Vol. II., p. 277. See also : "South Russian Labour Unions." Moscow, 1924.

brought before the Judicial Court, and it enjoyed all the privileges of a Government institution.*

In 1872, after the epidemic of cholera which took toll of 420 victims in the Krenholm works, the internal police was temporarily abolished ; very soon, however, the administration reintroduced it, and the same *starostas*, on whose removal the workmen had insisted, were reappointed to the internal police. This provoked a strike, which developed into a big riot, for which regular troops had to be called out. A State Commission, appointed to investigate the causes of the riot, reported that conditions of work in the Krenholm Manufacturing Company must be improved and that the internal police-court must be abolished for ever.

This strike and those in 1879 in St. Petersburg showed how greatly the ideas of negotiation through spokesmen and organisation of fellow-workmen within the industry were gaining ground. The workmen of the New cotton-mill, for instance, called a strike in 1879, one of their claims being the right to elect delegates, and the right of these delegates to be present in the office when payment of wages was made. This claim was immediately supported by the workers in other neighbouring mills (those belonging to Messrs. Shaw, Maltsev, Chester, Maxwell and others). Delegates were elected everywhere, they held joint meetings, issued appeals, and the movement spread over the cotton trade throughout the province.†

Most strike appeals were written by the workmen themselves in very simple idiomatic language, with the use of some revolutionary slogans. One leaflet,

* S. Farforovsky, "The Life of Workmen in the Krenholm Manufacturing Company's Works." *Archives*, Vol. II., p. 8.
† V. Svyatlovsky, "The Trade Union Movement in Russia." St. Petersburg, 1907, pp. 8–9.

for instance, was headed as follows : " The voice of workers suffering in the factory of the rascal Maxwell." In the text of the leaflet, which was issued during the 1879 strike, words like " rascal," " swine," etc., were mixed with slogans from the covers of revolutionary publications, like " Each for all and all for each." The practice of distributing leaflets or posting notices at the entrance gates or on the factory walls became very fashionable. The women employed in the Shapshall tobacco factory in St. Petersburg, for instance, during a strike in 1878 posted the following declaration on the factory gates : " We cannot stand any further reduction in our wages, for even the wages now being paid do not allow us to dress decently."*

The strike in the factory of Messrs. Surazhsky in Bielostock in 1882 proved that the idea of trade union organisation was present in the minds of the workers. During this strike for higher wages, the workers organised a fund, to which each of them contributed 50 kopeks weekly. This amounted to 240 roubles a week, which was of great help to the strikers. German workers engaged in the same trade also contributed to the fund and refused to blackleg their Jewish fellow-workers. The strike aroused great sympathy among the local Jewish population, and the owners of the factory were compelled to give in and accept the workers' terms.

The big strike of textile workers in the factory of Messrs. Morosov in Orekhovo-Zuevo in 1885, preceded by minor strikes in 1883 and 1884, had a marked influence upon the further development of the Russian Labour Movement. It made the Govern-

---

* G. Plekhanov, " The Revolutionary Movement of the Russian Workers." Moscow, 1919, p. 76. *Cf.* also V. Burtsev, *Byloe.* St. Petersburg, 1901, Vol. I., p. 182.

ment change its former attitude of non-interference in the relations of capital and labour, and take a part in labour legislation. The strike began on January 7th, 1885, and involved 4,000 workmen. The strikers presented to the Governor of the town of Vladimir a petition, written by themselves and almost entirely concerned with the economic aspects of their dissatisfaction.* The claims in the petition were, as a matter of fact, very moderate, as the exploitation of workers in the factory of Sava Morosov & Company, even according to official sources, was intolerable.

* P. Kantor, " The Morosov Strike in 1885," in *Archives*, Vol. II., p. 46.   The chief points of the petition were as follows :—

" 1. The factory owner has no legal right to impose exorbitant fines.   We workers insist herewith that the fine must not exceed 5 per cent. of each rouble earned.

" 2. Fines for absence from work must not exceed 1 rouble per day.   Such a fine for absence may only be imposed on condition that the owner guarantees to pay to each worker 40 kopeks per day, or 20 kopeks per shift if there is a shortage of work owing to machine repairs or a shortage of raw materials for work.

" 3. Notice, in accordance with the law, must be given by either side of the termination of a contract.   Full wages must be paid at the termination of a contract, without any reductions of fines or for any other reason.

" 4. Distribution of raw materials for work must take place in the presence of the workers' representatives, and their view of the quality of the materials must be taken into account. Wages for a new type of fabric must be calculated at time rates, and only after the workers have found out the quantity of the new fabric they can manufacture daily, may piecerates come into operation.

" 5. If contracts are not concluded between the parties, the State must regulate wages.   Wages must be paid monthly, on the 15th of each month, or on the first Saturday after that date.

" 6. The workers ought to have the right to elect their *starostas*.   The *starosta* must not be elected for more than three months.   Examination of the *artels'* account books which were entrusted with the provision of meals to the members of the *artel*, must be made every three months.

" In addition to this petition, a separate list will be made of the names of clerks in the administrative offices and of foremen, upon whose dismissal the workers insist."

Wages had been reduced by 25 per cent., fines reached 30 to 50 per cent. of wages. Mr. Litvinov-Falinsky, whose statement we can accept as an official recognition of the fact, says in his book on " Factory Legislation and Factory Inspection," that " fines and other deductions from wages reached sometimes 40 per cent., and these were used by the owners entirely at their own discretion."*

The factory owners did not want to negotiate at all with the strikers, and on the first day of the strike they telegraphed to the Minister of the Interior, Count Dimitry Tolstoy, asking for his help against the " rioters." Without waiting for any reply from him, they telegraphed again the next day to say that the " riot " was spreading. Count Dimitry Tolstoy, on receipt of these two telegrams, at once reported the strike to Alexander III., and the Emperor wrote on the report : " I fear that it is the work of anarchists. Please keep me informed of particulars of the strike which you receive from the Governor." After this endorsement of the report by the Tsar, the strike was dealt with entirely by the local police authorities. The latter, with the help of a regiment of Cossacks, and by means of arrests and the deportation of hundreds of strikers to their native villages, managed to bring the strike to an end in three weeks.†

The Court acquitted thirty-three of the arrested strikers, and the remaining seventeen workmen were sentenced only to three months' imprisonment.‡ The Editor of the *Moscow Gazette*, M. Katkov,

---

* V. P. Litvinov-Falinsky, "Factory Legislation and Factory Inspection." St. Petersburg, 1900, p. 61.

† *Archives*, Vol. II., p. 48.

‡ The reminiscences of the strike by Peter Moisseyenko, who was deported by the police to Siberia for five years, were published in the *Preletarskaya Revolutsia*. Moscow, 1924, No. 1 (24). See also : V. Ezhov. (S. Zederbaum) : "Peter Moisseyenko." Moscow, 1929.

expressed his disgust with the Court's decision in the words : " It is nothing but a friendly greeting to the labour cause ! " But this decision showed that there was justification for the workers' claims. The Government itself realised that the strike was a grave warning, and hastened to promulgate the Law of June 3rd, 1886, which incorporated all the demands put forward by the strikers.

The spirit of this Act did not differ much from other Acts which had occasionally been incorporated in Russian legislation before the Emancipation. The Law of June 3rd, 1886, was, however, undoubtedly a step towards the legal recognition of the right of workers to defend their own cause. They were allowed to have their own representatives or *starostas*, " on condition, however, that they did not show any affinity to the revolutionaries or seek to implicate other classes of the population."*

It is true that revolutionary and socialist ideas influenced the Russian Labour Movement from its very beginning, and we must give a short outline of their character, as the revolutionary and socialist movement developed in Russia under different conditions from those in Europe, and had a different scope and method.

First of all, the revolutionary movement in Russia was conceived as a socialist movement, and it could not be anything else but revolutionary. This can be

---

* *Cf.* V. P. Litvinov-Falinsky, *op. cit.*, pp. 22, 61 ; also P. Kantor in *Archives*, Vol. II., p. 44. The chief points of the Law of 1886 will be found in the Appendix, IV., p. 185. Previous to this Code there were, as we have seen, only occasional separate regulations, dealing, for example, with children's and women's work or night-work : the Act of 1882, for instance, prohibited the employment of children under 12, and restricted the working day to 8 hours for children of 12 to 15. The Act of 1885 prohibited night-work for women and young persons under 17 years of age. This Act was promulgated at the instance of the employers themselves owing to the depression in industry.

seen from the fact that even during the first revolutionary movement of the Decembrists in 1824, which was originated by officers of the Army and Navy, the influence of Saint-Simon, Fourier and Proudhon, as well as of the ideas of the French Revolution of 1789, was very great.

Secondly, the idea of democracy in Russia was inseparable from socialist and revolutionary ideas. " Socialism in Russia more than anywhere else represents democracy in general. This is what makes its political rôle much more important than it is in countries with a more and earlier developed democracy. . . . If in the English-speaking countries democracy is not socialistic . . . in Germany it is socialistic, though German socialism is endeavouring more and more to disavow its revolutionary beginnings. In Russia it is both socialistic and revolutionary."*

This could be seen in the early revolutionary movement, which had sprung up soon after the Emancipation, and which was called " *Narodnichestvo.*" The members of this movement went to live among the people (*narod*), among peasants and workers, in order to educate them, and propagate among them the idea of democracy. But soon, after numerous arrests of their members, they realised that only revolutionary methods could bring them nearer to the fulfilment of their ideas. Political terror was then admitted as one of the chief weapons of attack, and this split the *Narodnichestvo* into two groups : *Narodnaya Volya* (People's Will) and *Cherny Perediel* (Redistribution of the land). The former group became the prototype of the Social-Revolutionary Party, the latter still tried to adhere to the old

* P. Milyukov, " Russia and its Crisis." London : T. Fisher Unwin, 1905, pp. 335–339.

principles, and concentrated its activities amongst the industrial workmen. Out of their midst sprung up the social-democratic movement in Russia.*

The peculiarity of the Russian socialist movement lies also in the interpretation of Socialism itself. The doctrine of Socialism in Russia was always considered as a new kind of religious creed, not as merely a political movement. Russian socialists could never understand how Christianity, which they held to be anti-social in its emphasis on the individual and its negation of all materialistic conceptions, could be given a place in a socialist programme. Fabianism to them seemed as contradictory as Christian Science to many.

The latest period of the Russian socialist and revolutionary movement has its origin in Bakunin and Marx. The latter is greatly esteemed in Soviet Russia, the name of the former is hardly mentioned there. Bakunin's attitude towards revolutionary activities in Russia was as follows : " We must not teach the people," he said, " but incite it to revolt. The people have always revolted, but revolted badly, without unity and without results. We must introduce a plan, a system, an organisation into this disorderly revolt."† The three important branches of the Socialist movement in Russia (Social-Revolutionaries, Social-Democrats mensheviks and Social-Democrats bolsheviks) were greatly influenced by

* This division of the *Narodnichestvo* into two groups took place in 1879. The programme of the *Narodnaya Volya* is given in J. Mavor's book, " The Economic History of Russia," Vol. II., p. 118. The revolutionary movement of the Narodniki and the growth of revolutionary aspirations in Russia are described by M. Pokrovsky in his " Brief History of Russia." London, 1933, Vol. I., Pt. II. See also : " A Century of Political Life in Russia (1800–1896)." Edited in Russian by *V. Burtsev* and *S. Stepniak* (S. M. Kravchinsky) in London, 1897.

M. Pokrovsky, " Brief History of Russia," Vol. I., p. 183.

their ideas. These three groups had almost an identical final aim, and they differed only in method and in their interpretation of the particular phase of evolution on which Russian society had entered : the social-revolutionaries laid stress on the peasant movement, and had greater faith in the efficacy of " riots " and rebellions of the peasantry, than the social-democrats, who concentrated their attention on the growth of the Russian proletariat and denied terrorism as a revolutionary method.

The Russian Social-Democratic Party was founded in 1898, and has its origin in the society called *Osvobozhdenie Truda* (Emancipation of Labour), formed by George Plekhanov in 1883, and based on the principles of the First International. Plekhanov's followers were actually moderate Socialists, and represented the right wing of the Party ; Lenin represented its more extreme elements. At the Party Congresses in 1903 and 1907 these two groups were sharply divided on the question of tactics. Plekhanov's group formed the minority (*menshinstvo*), and Lenin's followers the majority (*bolshinstvo*), in the voting on a resolution on current events, and since that time the two groups became known as *mensheviki* and *bolsheviki*.*

The difference between the Russian Socialist organisations and those of Western Europe is to be traced also in the fact that Russian Socialists never had an opportunity to act as a legal political party. Even in the times of representative government in Russia (the Duma) they did not enjoy the status of a legal party, and were known as the social-demo-

---

* Compare M. N. Lyadov, " The History of the Russian Social-Democratic Party." Moscow, 1906. In 1925 it appeared under the heading : " How the Russian Communist Party (Bolshevik) was Formed."

cratic and *trudovaya* (labour) fractions. This illegal position had a great bearing on all their activities and methods of work. Whereas in Europe political parties relied on organisations whose strength was measured by their membership and funds, in Russia they were bound to rely only on mass meetings, resolutions passed at them, and upon secret " cells " in factories and workshops. The payment of membership fees was not compulsory, and therefore the funds of the Party and, as we shall see later, of trade unions as well, were always very meagre, and the Party depended on the financial backing of sympathisers and supporters such as Morosov, Krassin, Maxim Gorky, etc. Usually there were no regular elections of officers, and " responsible workers " of the Party were nominated and appointed by the Central Executive Committee (*Tsik*) of the Party.

In order to understand the method of mass propaganda and " political strikes " or mass strikes of a " political " nature, and all the efforts to keep the working masses in a state of agitation and at a high level of enthusiasm, which became so characteristic of the subsequent stages of the Russian Labour Movement, it is important to keep these special features of the Russian revolutionary movement in mind.

CHAPTER IV

THE RUSSIAN LABOUR MOVEMENT AT THE END OF THE NINETEENTH CENTURY

Disputes and " Group " Strikes—The Activities of the Russian Social-Democratic Party—The Famine of 1891—Demonstration Strikes—The Act of 1897—The Birth of Russian Trade Unionism—Revolutionary Propaganda—The Russian Labourer and the Character of the Russian Labour Movement.

THE Act of June 3rd, 1886, to which we referred in the previous chapter, and which was known as " the First Russian Labour Code," signified that the Russian Government had changed its policy of non-interference in the relation of capital and labour, and had adopted a policy of intervention, which in its early stage was liberal in character, but became reactionary at the end of the nineteenth century. The conditions of the workers at that time began to worsen : economic exploitation by the masters increased. The factory inspectors, who were at first under the control of the local government (*zemstvo*), and who were able to carry out a good deal of philanthropic work, were soon reduced to the ineffective level of central Government officials, and were even employed as police agents.*

* The industrial population of Russia consisted at that time of over one and a half million people. Its growth since the emancipation was as follows :—

1861–1870	.	.	. 797,649 workmen
1871–1880	.	.	. 945,597 ,,
1881–1890	.	.	. 1,160,771 ,,
1891–1900	.	.	. 1,637,595 ,,

A. V. Pogozhev, " Statistics of Industrial Workers in Russia." St. Petersburg, 1906, p. 16.

The strike movement was increasing, and became more systematic with the marked increase in the solidarity of the workers. In the course of most of the disputes strike committees were formed, and the majority of all recorded strikes were the so-called " group " strikes, which embraced several factories in the same branch of industry. Attempts were made also to create more or less permanent labour organisations, but most of them did not last long, and were soon traced by the police. The activities of the Russian social-democrats in this direction were, perhaps, more successful than the separate attempts of workmen. The Social-Democratic Group—" The Emancipation of Labour "—created secret " cells " in factories, and supported the strikers out of funds partly collected among the workers themselves and partly subscribed by private individuals.*

The famine of 1891–92, which affected chiefly the grain-producing area in the south and the Province of the Lower Volga, had also a certain psychological effect upon peasants and workmen. It created a feeling of national solidarity among them, and

* At the end of the nineteenth century factory " cells " and secret committees of the Social-Democratic party already existed in St. Petersburg, Vladimir, Tula, Kazan, Kharkov, Kiev, Rostov on Don, Vilna, Moscow, Warsaw, Lodz, Odessa, Samara and Saratov. These committees consisted mainly of the Russian intelligentsia. The working-class membership was comparatively insignificant. But in spite of this the propaganda of socialist ideas found great response among the workers. This was due partly to the fact that " the Russian workers were brought into the factories straight from the plough. . . . They lacked political and economic training, and therefore they were ready to grasp eagerly the first slogan brought to them by the socialists." (P. Maslov, " The Development of National Wealth," cited in the " Economic Development and the Class War," p. 656.)

The Minister of the Interior (Goremykin) attached to his Report to Nicholas II., the following copy of the balance sheet of the " Emancipation of Labour " for 1896, which throws light on the

provided them with good social and political training. Voluntary contributions poured in to every local newspaper agent from factories and villages. Newspapers in which information regarding the famine-stricken area was given were read aloud at every village meeting. The present writer, then a little boy, was surprised to find, when wandering from village to village with a pile of newspapers collecting contributions, how great was the belief of the illiterate peasants in the printed word. It did not matter if it were a Government publication, a newspaper, or a revolutionary leaflet.

The famine of 1891–92 had a marked effect on Russian revolutionary circles as well. Some of the revolutionaries came to the conclusion that propaganda of Socialist ideas, based on the everyday economic needs of the population, might be more successful than the purely theoretic teaching of Socialism to more advanced workmen. This attitude of the revolutionaries showed itself more clearly later in the activities of the so-called " Economists." Their

part played in the strike movement by the revolutionary intelligentsia at that time :—

Financial Statement of the " Emancipation of Labour " from December 1st, 1895, to December 1st, 1896.

	Roubles.
Propaganda, literature and printing .	2223·36
Strikes	3203
Subsidies	1943·60
Organisation, expenses of delegate to International Socialist Congress . .	1021·80
Loans	238
Help to the Polish workers . . .	120

Total 8749·76

These items of expenditure speak for themselves, but to the Minister of the Interior they seemed to be of great importance and a menace to the safety of the State. (" Reports of the Ministry of the Interior to Nicholas II.," Vol. I., Paris, 1909, p. 17.)

efforts were directed to the concentration of the strike movement round the everyday needs of the workers and their economic exploitation. The " Economists " held that only in the process of this struggle for better conditions would the Russian workers acquire class consciousness and be prepared to adopt the ideas of Socialism. They did not believe that the development of Russian trade unionism would follow the path of syndicalism, and based their views on the practice of German and English trade unions. They held that in Russia, as in England, trade unions would be more successful if they began " as a combination of wage earners struggling for rather more tolerable conditions of life " in order to proceed to " the Socialist ideal of the complete emancipation of the working class."*

After the famine of 1891–92, there set in a period of prosperity which lasted until 1898. The strike movement in this period changed its character ; it passed on to the offensive. The percentage of disputes for higher wages and shorter hours was much higher than of those due to resistance to the reduction of wages and longer hours of work. But the majority of disputes still ended in favour of the employers, and, in spite of their persistent struggle for better conditions, the workers were subjected to intolerable exploitation. The working day in most factories was twelve hours or more. In 20 per cent. of all enterprises night work was the rule, and workers were employed even on Sundays. Real wages, owing to the rise in prices and the almost stationary level of nominal wages, were very low ; a man's average wage was equal to 187·6 roubles per year, while

* C. M. Lloyd, " Trade Unionism." London Ed., 1921, p. 77. Later on the " Economists " joined the right wing of the Social Democrats, known as the " Mensheviks."

women received only half this amount and young persons only a third.*

The failure of the separate strikes to win better conditions and especially shorter hours of work in all factories, led the workers to think that only a Government Act regulating hours of labour could be of use to them. In order, therefore, to call the attention of the Government and of the working masses to the necessity for regulation, they decided to initiate " demonstration strikes." This new type of strike was started by the St. Petersburg workers in 1895, and the movement soon spread all over the country. The strikers everywhere insisted on the introduction of a $10\frac{1}{2}$ hours' working day (from 7 a.m. to 7 p.m., with an interval of $1\frac{1}{2}$ hours for dinner) and a shorter working day on Saturday (from 7 a.m. to 2 p.m.). The strikes were carried on quite peacefully and conflicts with the police were everywhere avoided. It was arranged in advance that a strike should be called off by the strike committee, when it became evident that the employers were putting up vigorous resistance and were not willing to meet the workers' claims.†

All these endeavours of workers had a certain

---

* D. Koltsov, " The Russian Labour Movement," in " The Liberation Movement." St. Petersburg, 1909, Vol. I., p. 187.

† During 1895–97 there were, according to official data, 303 strikes of this nature, involving 90,162 workers. Private information of the revolutionary organisations gave a much higher figure. The Ministry of the Interior, in one of its secret circulars, admitted that the economic conditions of the workers were very bad, and that hours of work were very long. It also agreed that it was not surprising that the workers came out on strike, but it attributed the spread of the movement exclusively to the agitation and propaganda of the revolutionary organisations, " The Emancipation of Labour " and " The Labour Union," and believed that the strong discipline shown by the workers was due to the influence of these organisations. See V. Kolpensky, " Factory Strikes and Factory Legislation," in the *Archives*, Vol. II., p. 40 ; " Russian Laws and Labourer." Stuttgart, 1002, p. 45.

influence on the Government, who produced on June 2nd, 1897, an Act, according to which the working day was fixed at $11\frac{1}{2}$ hours, and, if the work was done in two shifts, at 10 hours.

There were certain classes of workers which were inclined to see in the promulgation of the Act of June 2nd, 1897, not so much the result of an organised struggle of workers as the hand of God. The workmen of the Krenholm Manufacturing Company in Narva, for instance, on hearing the news of the publication of the Act, held a thanksgiving service to render thanks to God for having helped the Petersburg workers to obtain a shorter working day for them.*

Unfortunately the Act of 1897, owing to its vagueness, was capable of very wide interpretation, and since it was not accompanied by provisions to ensure its proper working, it soon became practically a dead letter. Employers in general regulated the working of overtime and of shifts at their own discretion, and this created a new series of strikes, of which the object was to compel the employers to comply with the new law. The majority of such claims were conceded by the employers, though, whenever they could, the police attributed the strikes to the influence of the intelligentsia and revolutionaries. This reminds me that some of the textile workers in my native village asked me to give them advice and help in inducing the owners of some big silk mills to abide by the letter of the law and to introduce a ten-hours' working day in all workshops working on two shifts. I expressed the opinion that such a claim might have every

---

* V. Astrov, cited in the "Economic Developuentete," Vol. II., p. 320. A detailed analysis of the Act of June 2nd, 1897, is given by Peter Struve in the *Narodnoye Khozyaistvo*. St. Petersburg, March 1902.

chance of succeeding, and the workers, after the refusal by the employers to satisfy their demand, called a strike. It did not last long. The owners agreed to institute the ten-hours' working day, but voiced their suspicion that there must be among the workers, who were mostly peasants from neighbouring villages, some outside elements stirring up the trouble. The police authorities were convinced that this was the case, and sent agents to search the strikers, their dwellings and any suspected " outside elements." But their efforts failed to disclose any " initiators " of revolutionary activity among the peaceful peasants.

The success of the organised struggle for a shorter working day, and the need for its defence, strengthened the workmen's desire to effect some kind of permanent professional organisation. How great was the interest towards trade union organisation is shown by the following fact : a group of textile workers in my native village, about twenty miles from Moscow, decided to issue a hand-written journal called *The Labourer*. Having failed to communicate with the Social-Democratic Party or with one of its " propagandists," and to find contributors for the journal, they borrowed from me for reading Mr. and Mrs. Webb's " Industrial Democracy," which at that time was already translated into Russian, and asked me to summarise for the journal Part II. on " Trade Union Functions."

It was in this period, or a little before, that Russian trade unionism had its birth, though it was not yet known under that name. It was to be found in such organisations as the " labour unions," " labour committees," " strike committees " and " labour societies," which were set up in the process of the struggle with the employers for better conditions, as

well as in *starostas*, *artels*, and the various friendly
societies for mutual help among the workers.*

Strike committees (often called Strike Funds or
Strike Treasuries) were actually the main type of
labour organisation after the series of strikes in
1895–97. They were not only concerned with the
casual organisation of a strike and with helping the
strikers, but aimed at building a permanent organisation within the industry. Several attempts were
made to create a central body which should unite all
existing labour organisations in a given locality or
industry, but this aim was not achieved until the
revolutionary period of 1905.†

If the chief characteristics of the Russian labourer

---

* Friendly societies for mutual help had actually existed
among Russian workers since the beginning of the nineteenth
century. The St. Petersburg compositors, for instance, formed a
friendly society in 1838, and those of Moscow in 1869, while in
the eighties and nineties such societies sprang up in the South of
Russia also. (D. Grinevich, "The Trade Union Movement in
Russia." St. Petersburg, 1908, p. 10.)

In Poland and the Baltic Provinces societies for mutual help
grew rapidly in the tailoring trade and other branches of home
industry. The structure and aims of these societies were very
different from those of the labour organisations which came into
being as a result of the strike movement. They were formed only
for mutual help, and excluded any idea of interference in the relations
of labour and capital. Their membership was mixed in character,
and the employer was often the President or an honorary member.
Money belonging to the societies was usually put in charge of the
administration, but its distribution was decided upon by the members
themselves.

Later, with the growth of trade unions, these societies changed
their character and either disappeared gradually or developed into
proper trade unions or consumers' co-operative societies. A short
survey of the co-operative movement in Russia will be found in the
Supplement to this book.

† In Russian Poland and Latvia, the process of building permanent organisations out of the strike committees was further advanced, and by 1900 from 20 to 40 per cent. of the Jewish working
population were already united. The revolutionary organisation
known as the "Bund," which was created in 1897, was largely
supported by the strike committees, and based its activities on
them. (P. Grinevich, *op. cit.*, p. 18.)

during the period under consideration are reviewed, it will be found that the majority of Russian workmen were mainly peaceful peasants engaged in industry. They did not, in fact, lose their connection with the countryside, and regarded themselves not as a purely proletarian working-class, but as peasants and members of their village community. But some Russian economists believed that Russia had " a large industrial proletariat, which belonged only nominally to the peasantry, and was as far removed from the land as the proletariat in Europe, with the same degree of insecurity."* And the investigations of factory inspectors seemed to confirm this opinion. They showed that in the Moscow Province from 72 to 82 per cent. of workers had lost their ties with the countryside, and did not leave the factories during the seasons of agricultural operations in order to work on the land.† This may have been the case ; but it must be remembered that the investigations in question were mainly concerned with the aristocracy of the Russian working-class engaged in the mechanical and printing trades. The majority of workmen in the Moscow Province belonged to the textile industry. These used to leave the factories during the seasons of agricultural operations, and kept a close connection with the countryside. " The hand-loom weavers remained peasants to a much greater extent : only 6 per cent. in the woollen industry, and hardly 4 per cent. in the cotton industry worked in the factory all the year round."‡

" While in the metal industry, especially in Petrograd, a layer of hereditary proletarians was crystal-

* M. Tugan-Baranovsky, " The Russian Factory." Ed. 1922, pp. 338, etc.
† A Pogozhev, " Statistics of Industrial Workers in Russia." St. Petersburg, 1906, p. 184.
‡ M. Pokrovsky, " Brief History of Russia," Vol. I., p. 210.

lised out, having made a complete break with the country, in the Urals the prevailing type was half-proletarian, half-peasant.*

This close connection of the Russian workmen with the countryside survived the first Revolution of 1905, and even the second Revolution of 1917. " Up to the present our industrial working population," wrote L. M. Pumpyansky in the *Economist* in 1922, " considers its occupation in industry as of secondary importance and tries by all means not to lose its ties with the countryside. The labouring masses are still in their spirit and in their interests, peasants," and they consider their work in the factories to be only a temporary occupation and quite subordinate to their work on the land.†

* Leon Trotsky, "The History of the Russian Revolution." London, 1934, Vol. I., p. 33.
† L. M. Pumpyansky, "Industrial Labour" in the *Economist*. Moscow, 1922, No. 1, p. 110.

CHAPTER V

POLICE SOCIALISM IN RUSSIA

The Industrial Crisis of the late Nineteenth Century and the Discontent in the Country—The Law of January 10th, 1903—Zubatov and his Organisation—Professor Ozerov and the Revolutionaries—The Zubatov Organisation in St. Petersburg and in the Provinces.

THE period of industrial prosperity in Russia came to an end in 1898–99, and the strike movement began to weaken : the number of workers involved in disputes in 1901 came down to one-third of that in 1899. The character of strikes changed also : they became a desperate fight for the workers' very existence. Unemployment increased and there were several riots, which were dealt with by the police and troops. Revolutionary agitation also increased, and a series of organised street demonstrations impressed on the mind of the public the existence of grievances which had not been realised before.*

" In June, 1896, St. Petersburg was roused by a startling movement of workmen, the like of which it had never before seen. The workers in twenty-two cotton factories of the northern capital, numbering more than thirty thousand, organised something like a general strike. There were no visible signs of any preparatory propaganda by the socialists, and no ' intellectual ' leaders made themselves prominent. All the proclamations and other papers published during the strike were written by the men themselves, in a plain, half-educated language. To be sure, small circles of workmen, reading socialist pamphlets under

* See Appendix V., p. 187.

the direction of young students, had always existed.
But these were few, and could by no means account
for the large spread of the strike. The socialists
themselves vowed that they were taken by surprise,
and they bitterly upbraided themselves for not
having been better prepared to take advantage of
the opportunity. The demands formulated by the
strikers were of a strictly professional—*i.e.*, economic
—character. They were so moderate and sensible
that immediately after the strike became known the
Ministry of Finance ordered the owners of the
manufactures to remedy the most crying abuses.
The methods employed by the strikers were quite
peaceful ; no violence was resorted to, and the chief
means of protest were simply staying at home."*

The movement produced a great impression on both
the Government and the revolutionaries. But the
Government stupidly resisted the idea of granting
the workers the right to strike and to form
their own organisations : it was afraid that the
Russian workers might come into touch with the
international labour movement, which would be
" hardly useful to Russia. Attention must be paid,"
according to a Government document, " not to the
creation of purely labour organisations and the
isolation of the workers from the rest of the population," but to their subordination to Government
control. Even Count S. Witte, the Minister of
Finance, whose " liberalism " was causing alarm in
the Ministry of the Interior, did not propose any
more drastic remedy than a law that would
" guarantee order." And such a law was brought
in on June 10th, 1903, when the workers were
granted the right to elect candidates for the position
of *starosta*, though the final selection was left to the

* P. Milyukov, " Russia and its Crisis." London, 1905, p. 480.

discretion of the factory administration, who might even refuse to consider the candidates nominated, and demand that a new set should be elected. This law was practically reduced to a farce by restricting the age of candidates to over twenty-five years, giving every workman the right to enter into direct negotiation with the administration, avoiding the mediation of *starostas*, and prohibiting joint meetings of *starostas*. This left the workers, as before, at the mercy of the employers.*

Another Act, which was published a few days before on June 2nd, and which dealt with compensation of workers in case of accident and pensions to their families, also was unsatisfactory. It applied to a very limited number of workers ; the definition of industrial risks in it was very vague ; and rates of compensation and of pensions were very low. After being in operation for two years, it was found to be costing industry only 1 per cent. of the annual wages bill.†

It took two years for the Ministry of Finance to work out these laws in the hope that they would satisfy public opinion and would guarantee order, and control over the growing Labour Movement. But the Labour Movement seemed more menacing to the Minister of the Interior, who was responsible for keeping order in the country and who put little trust in the gentle " liberal " measures of his colleague. The Ministry of the Interior contemplated quite different means of coping with the problem. It initiated a scheme, which has come to be known as *Zubatovshchina*, and which was actually nothing but " police socialism."

---

* " Materials on the Labour Question." Edited by the *Osvobozh-denie*. Stuttgart, 1903, Vol. II., pp. xiv., 8 and 23.
† A. Bykov, " Factory Legislation," p. 218.

S. Zubatov, the founder of the new organisation, a former revolutionary who became head of the Moscow Secret Police (*Okhrana*), conceived the idea, according to his own statement, of " opposing the mass labour movement which the revolutionaries had created."* The Moscow Secret Police were quite well aware of the aspirations of the working masses, for Zubatov, while being connected with the *Okhrana*, was in touch with the Social-Democratic Organisation in Moscow, and had even helped them to set up a new illegal printing plant in place of one which had been raided by the police. He knew that the working masses were actually without any strong leadership ; that the labour organisations were still in an embryonic stage of development and extremely weak ; and that revolutionary propaganda was successful only among the more advanced workers. It was well known, also, that the workers were eager for legal organisations of their own, which would unite them in their struggle against economic exploitation. The Ministry of the Interior therefore decided to set about controlling the Labour Movement, not by creating independent labour organisations, but through administrative channels, by founding legal labour organisations under the guidance and supervision of the Secret Police.†

* V. Svyatlovsky, " The Trade Union Movement." St. Petersburg, 1907, p. 54.

† The origin of this idea can be traced as far back as 1899, when Trepov, the Chief of the Moscow police, in a Report to the Grand Duke Sergius, stated that repression was effective only at the stage when revolutionaries were preaching the gospel of Socialism to the masses, and that it was not sufficient when they were exploiting the everyday needs of the workers for their own ends. Some positive measures on the part of the administration then become necessary. He also thought it would be good to treat any strike as a political offence, and recommended that all dealings with strikers should be taken out of the hands of the factory inspectors, who were subordinated to the Ministry of Finance. " Labour's Thought," 1899, No. 6, Appendix.

Zubatov, guided by all these considerations, started in Moscow, in 1901, an organisation under the name of the " Society of Workers in the Moscow Mechanical Trades." He sought for members among the more advanced workmen in evening and Sunday classes, and suggested they should ask the well-known Professor Ozerov to prepare a draft of rules for the new society. Professor Ozerov, together with Mr. V. E. Den, a lecturer at the University of Moscow, agreed, after some hesitation, to do so, and both took an active part in the organisation and work of the new society. " The scientists did not notice, or did not want to notice, that behind their backs some dirty work was being done."*

The original draft rules underwent such a change in the Ministry of the Interior that the authors could hardly recognise them. All the names of members of the Council (Soviet) of the Society, for instance, were to be approved by the Moscow Chief of Police. The Society was granted the right to have honorary members, but only the following persons were eligible : chief factory inspectors, representatives of the police, and of the factory administrations, and priests. The Society, according to the rules, must not give any relief to strikers, and unemployment benefit was allowed only in those cases where employment was lost not through the worker's fault. Fortunately, most of these restrictions remained a dead letter, and during the first big strike in the nail factory of Goujon, the Society decided, in spite of the ban, to give material help to the strikers, and the police could not prevent this.

The new Society grew rapidly : the workers were proud to have for the first time a legal organisation of their own. Its activities during the first six months

* V. Svyatlovsky, *op. cit.*, p. 57.

of its existence were purely educational : lectures were delivered by such authorities as Professor Paul Vinogradoff, Professor A. Manuilov, A. Vesselovsky, B. Sobolevsky, the editor of the Liberal newspaper, *Russkiya Viedomosti*, and others.

Professor Ozerov organised an investigation into the conditions of work and life of the Moscow workers, which revealed appalling factory conditions. " The narratives of workers at our meetings," says Professor Ozerov, " have shown us a very depressing picture of the workers' lives. Everything depends on the master. He must be given a bribe if one wants a job ; he can dismiss all who fail to greet him. Fines for being even five minutes late are very heavy. But what is even more disgusting is the practice of searching the person. A worker is searched every time he leaves the factory : sometimes he is asked at the gate to unfasten his suit or to take off his boots, even in cold and frosty weather. ' We are searched because we are suspected,' wrote a worker, ' but when some of the members of the administration are suspected, or when they have appropriated a large sum of money, it is attributed to kleptomania.'

" In 1899 the administration of a factory issued an order that the lavatory was to be used only four times a day. For additional use a fine of 10 kopeks would be imposed. This rule was approved by the factory inspector and was in force up to 1901. Then a factory inspector, Obukhovsky, refused to give his sanction to it, but the administration still kept a clerk sitting at the entrance to the lavatory to register the names of those who used it more than four times. The next morning the offenders would be fined at the rate of 10 kopeks for each additional visit to the lavatory. ' One must,' wrote the workmen to Professor Ozerov, ' devise all kinds of ways of satisfying this natural need, and often it is done in the workshop, as the offender cannot afford to pay the fine '."*

The peaceful educational meetings of the Society did not last long, for the workers were anxious to discuss their economic needs and the means for satisfying them. The policy of the Council of the Society in prohibiting all discussion of the strike movement, even in their own trade, greatly irritated the members. At the same time, the textile workers, who in Moscow were more numerous than workers in the mechanical trades, were naturally annoyed at not being granted the right to create a legal society of their own, as were also workers in other trades. Meanwhile the enmity felt by the Social-Democratic Party against Professor Ozerov broke out into open propaganda to prevent the workers joining the Society, and criticism was levelled at all the activities of the Council of the Society and especially against Professor Ozerov himself. The latter was obliged to appeal to an arbitration court, headed by Professor Paul Vinogradoff and W. Skalon, of the *Russkiya Viedomosti*.†

The arbitration court approved of Professor Ozerov's activities. It recommended that the work of the Society should be continued and developed on a more systematic basis, and that full advantage

---

* I. Ozerov, "The Labour Question in Russia." Moscow, 1906, p. 211.

† The reasons which the Social-Democratic Party put forward against participation in the Society's work were as follows :—

(*a*) The lectures, owing to strict censorship, did not convey to the workers correct explanations of facts.

(*b*) The Society was deprived of the right of taking any practical steps in the workers' interests.

(*c*) The main purpose of general meetings of the Society was the creation of a favourable attitude among the workers towards Government policy.

should be taken of the legal labour organisation so that the workers should not be left at the mercy of the local police.*

The boycott of the meetings by the leaders of the Social-Democratic Party facilitated the work of the *agents provocateurs*, since the absence of opposition at the general meetings enabled them to exercise a greater influence on the working masses. " The Social Democrats, by their mistaken tactics in the economic struggles of the workers and by their exaggerated fear of any kind of legal labour organisation, gave to the police agents a chance to fill the places which were theirs."† And the police did not miss their chance. They provoked, for instance, a strike in the nail factory of Goujon, a French subject, with the object of demonstrating to the workers by their victory that the local police administration had their interests at heart. This would also provide an opportunity for the police to rehabilitate themselves in the eyes of the workers, who were displeased at the passive attitude of the Council of the Society to the strike movement. The police, at the same time, hoped to rid themselves during the strike of the more disquieting elements among the workers.‡

All these expectations were defeated, however, in the early days of the strike, for the workers immediately took matters into their own hands. They organised regular help for the strikers out of the

(*d*) The general meetings were a kind of trap for workers with more advanced views, who could be traced afterwards and prosecuted for the views which they had expressed.

(*e*) The existence of only one Society, that of the mechanical workers, created disunity among the workers and put the mechanical workers in a privileged position.

* *Ibid.*, p. 218.

† D. Grinevich, " The Trade Union Movement," p. 25.

‡ An adverse interpretation of Zubatov's success will be found in the book of M. N. Lyadov, " The History of the Russian Social-Democratic Party." Moscow, Ed. 1925, p. 361.

funds of the Society of Mechanical Workers : they
put pickets at the factory gates and persuaded the
peasants, who had been called in by the factory
administration, not to blackleg, but to return home
at the expense of the Society.

This was the first time the Ministry of the Interior
had failed to control a strike through the local secret
police.   A second defeat followed closely on the first.
The textile workers of Moscow insisted on their right
to form a legal organisation of their own, and in 1902
such an organisation, similar to the Society of the
Mechanical Trades, was set up.   The Metropolitan of
Moscow, the Chief of Police, the editor of the
reactionary paper *Moskovskiya Viedomosti* and the
employers were among the honorary members of the
Society.   But all this did not prevent the textile
workers from going their own way and, leaving aside
purely educational activities, they set about dis-
cussing the wages question.   It was agreed to send
representatives of the Society all over the Moscow
Province to negotiate a new scale of wages with the
employers.   But the negotiations failed, and as a
result, strikes soon broke out in practically every
textile factory in the district, and the Ministry of the
Interior could not cope with the movement.   " It
has bitten off more than it can chew," said Professor
Ozerov.*

* One of the leaders of the textile workers was a certain Afanassiev,
who was suspected by the revolutionaries of being an *agent provocateur*.   But these suspicions were hardly justified.   The present
writer used to meet Afanassiev among the textile workers, and
knew his previous history well.   He was an advanced peasant-
workman, a natural leader.   He was not a socialist, but held very
advanced democratic views and, as he was the chairman of the
meetings held by Professor Ozerov, he was obliged to deal with the
police.   For this he was accused of being in the pay of the police.
Afanassiev trusted neither the revolutionaries nor the police, and
preferred to go his own way.   He did not mind when young revolutionaries tried to explain Marx's " Communist Manifesto " to the

Zubatov organisations had also been set up in the provinces. In Minsk, for instance, the local secret police organised a " Jewish Independent Labour Party," which aimed at pursuing the purely economic struggle by legal means and without any disloyalty to the Government. In Odessa, the police agent, Shayevich, caused a good deal of trouble when the strike movement organised by him developed into a general strike (July 1903), with the strikers in complete control of the town. The Director of the Police Department, Zvolyansky, confessed in his Report that the movement, initiated by the Ministry of the Interior with the sole purpose of counteracting revolutionary propaganda, had failed entirely, and that the Government could not now stop the Labour Movement from spreading in all big industrial centres.*

Experiments with Zubatov's organisations in St. Petersburg did not meet with much success, as the more advanced and the intelligent workers of the capital had no faith in the sincerity of the police, who offered to set up legal labour organisations with their own agents in charge. But an attempt was nevertheless made in St. Petersburg, though in this case it was the Ministry of Finance and not the Ministry of the Interior which initiated it. In 1904 a friendly society of workers in the mechanical trades was inaugurated with great pomp at a ceremony presided over by the Archbishop Ornatsky. The founder of the Society was a worker named M. Ushakov, and the Governor of St. Petersburg,

---

illiterate textile workers, but he tactfully declined any interference by them in the economic struggles of the workers, preferring to retain the leadership in his own hands.

* I. Ozerov, *op. cit.*, p. 237. See also *Krasny Arkhiv*, Moscow, 1922, Vol. I., p. 289: "New Light on the Zubatovshchina," by S. Piantkovsky.

General Fulon, made a speech, while the Ministry of Finance was represented by the factory inspector, V. P. Litvinov-Falinsky. A vote of thanks was passed to the latter for financial help given to the Society. The Society began to publish a paper called the *Labour Gazette*, with the help of a subsidy from the Ministry of Finance. It even opened branches in Moscow under the name of " Independent Social Labour Party " and " Central Labour Union." But its activities were very slight, and it had no great influence among the workers. Later, in 1906, Ushakov brought a libel action against two of his fellow-workers, who had called him a " thief and provocateur " for his activities in the Society ; but both were acquitted.*

Such were the main outlines of the intervention of the police in the natural development of the Russian Labour Movement. The absence of a strong permanent organisation amongst the workmen, mistrust on the part of revolutionaries of any kind of legal labour representation and organisation, and their sharp criticism and boycott of the honest and sincere, but naive, attempts of Professor Ozerov and other scientists to take full advantage of legal labour organisation—all this paved the way for such an enterprise as the *Zubatovshchina*.

Some writers on Russian problems were inclined to attribute the possibility of such an enterprise to the personal qualities of Zubatov alone. There was no doubt that Zubatov was a capable *agent provocateur*, but we must not overlook the fact that the whole system of the Russian police was behind him.

The *Zubatovshchina* was not a purely modern or Russian invention. In the early European history of labour regulation, and especially in the times of

* V. Svyatlovsky, *op. cit.*, p. 95.

serfdom and forced labour, we can find similar intervention and espionage. And in the history of trade
unionism of Europe we can trace the elements of
" police socialism." The difference is only that in
Europe it had not taken such an extreme form as in
Russia.

The *Zubatovshchina* counted on the "patriarchal
relations between masters and servants," on the
illiteracy of the peasants and workmen and on the
influence of the Church on the population. The
patriarchal relations between employers and workmen, and the ignorance of the working masses, were
largely exploited by the police, in order to counteract
the influence of revolutionaries on the Russian
Labour Movement. The ecclesiastical influence was
not at first utilised for that purpose. This source of
spiritual life, and of influence on the labouring
masses, was taken into account later on, and led to
the birth of another experiment, started by " Father
Gapon," who did not realise that he was lighting the
spark which would bring about the Revolution of
1905.

CHAPTER VI

FATHER GAPON AND THE REVOLUTION OF 1905

The Russo-Japanese War—Fear of a General Strike—Father Gapon
—The Patilov Strike—The Gapon Society—January 9th, 1905,
and the Workers' Petition—The Russian Social-Democrats and the
Gapon Society—The Commission of Senator Shidlovsky—The
Declaration of the Labour Delegation—Banquets of Liberals—
The Revolution of 1905—The Characteristic Features of the Russian
Labour Movement—The First Soviet of Workers' Deputies.

THE discontent of the population with the Russo-Japanese War, the anti-war manifestations and the spread of the strike movement made the position of the Russian Government at the beginning of the twentieth century very uneasy. It was ready to support and assist any new scheme likely to prevent or allay the outburst of revolt or the declaration of a general strike.

And such a scheme was contemplated this time by the chaplain of one of the prisons in St. Petersburg, Gapon. This man, during his student years at the Theological College, became acquainted with some of the revolutionary publications, and was very much attracted by those of Tolstoy, which at that time were prohibited in Russia. Impressed with the illiteracy, misery, and discontent of the Russian workers, Gapon came to the conclusion that their sufferings would be relieved if they were more educated and united.

For this purpose he organised a small group of workmen with a programme, which reminds us very much of " Pleasant Sunday Afternoon " meetings for working men, and which included the study of social and labour problems. The group soon became, to Gapon's own amazement, very popular, and it was decided to convert it into the " Gapon Society of St. Petersburg Workers." In 1904 its membership was already 1,200. The Society devoted itself mainly to the discussion of current events, and to the reading of illegal revolutionary books. The members of the Society even discussed the problem of introducing an eight-hour working day and a constitutional form of government in Russia.

By the end of 1904 the employers became highly suspicious of the growth of the Gapon Society (there were at that time already 7,000 or 8,000 members), and did not approve of the participation of their workers in the activities of the Society. The administration of the Putilov ironworks went so far as to dismiss some of its members employed by them, and this was the signal for a general strike in St. Petersburg on January 7th, 1905.

The following demands were presented during this strike :

1. An eight-hour working day.
2. A new scale of wages worked out in consultation with workers' representatives.
3. Appointment of Arbitration Courts, consisting of an equal number of workers and employers.
4. A minimum wage for unskilled workers (1 rouble per day).
5. Abolition of overtime except where it is indispensable. (Double pay to be given for overtime worked.)
6. Full pay for imperfect work if this is due to no fault of the workman.
7. A minimum wage for unskilled women workers (70 kopeks a day). The establishment of *crèches* for children.
8. More efficient medical aid in factories.
9. Improvement in the sanitary conditions of work.
10. No reprisals for participation in strikes.

11. Abolition of searching of the person and of fines for coming late to work.

12. Payment of half wages during illness. Medical treatment at the factory's expense.*

It will be seen from this programme that the movement was a protest against the exploitation of the workers. " It was a mass movement, and the revolutionary parties did not participate in it. If their spokesmen appeared on platforms, they only had success with small groups of the more advanced workers."† The strikers were so sure of the righteousness of their cause, that when the idea of going straight to the Tsar was put forward at meetings of Gapon's Society, it met with immediate approval, though Gapon himself was somewhat reluctant.‡

On the eve of this great drama, the representatives of the workers, together with Father Gapon, sent a warning to the Government authorities of the proposed march, and Gapon sent his secretary to Prince Svyatopolk-Mirsky, the Minister of the Interior, with a letter of which copies had been widely circulated among the public.§

* D. Koltsov, " The Russian Labour Movement in the Liberation Movement," Vol. II., p. 189.

† L. Gurevich, " The People's Movement in St. Petersburg, January 9th, 1905," in *Byloe*, 1906, No. 1, p. 205.

‡ " The idea of presenting a petition to the Tsar was anything but revolutionary. It was rather traditional, and though there have been in our history instances of meeting the demands of the people, as they were met on January 9th (the Tsar Alexis, for example. in the seventeenth century made his soldiers slaughter the crowd that came to his palace in Kolomenskoye), there have also been instances of a different reception. A quarter of a century ago (1878) a deputation of working-men was quietly received in the Anichkov Palace by the then heir-apparent (Alexander III.)." P. Milyukov, " Russia and its Crisis." London, 1905, T. Fisher Unwin, p. 536.

§ The contents of the letter were as follows :—

" Your High Excellency. The workers and inhabitants of St. Petersburg of different classes desire to see the Tsar at two in

The petition which the marchers to the Winter Palace were going to present to the Tsar was characteristic of the psychology and outlook of the Russian people at that time, and reflected all the sorrows and sufferings of the workers. The authorship of the petition is unknown. Its contents were as follows :

" Your Majesty ! We, the workmen and citizens of St. Petersburg, our wives, children and parents, have come to Your Majesty to beg for justice and protection. We are all paupers, we are oppressed and overburdened with work ; we are often insulted for no reason, we are not regarded as human beings but are treated as slaves ; we suffer and we have to bear our sufferings silently. We are driven further and further into the abyss of poverty, anarchy and ignorance; we are strangled by despotism and tyranny, so that we can breathe no longer. We have no strength at all, Your Majesty. Our patience is exhausted. We are approaching that stage when death is better than the continuance of our intolerable sufferings.

" And now, we have knocked off work and we have announced to our employers that we shall not go back to work until they satisfy us. We want only a little. We want

the afternoon of January 22 (9) in the square of the Winter Palace, in order to lay before him personally their needs and those of the whole Russian people. The Tsar has nothing to fear. As representative of the Union of Russian Factory Workers, I can assure him of this, and my fellow workers and comrades, even those alleged to belong to revolutionary groups, guarantee the inviolability of his person. Let him come as the true Tsar with courage in his heart to his people and receive from our hands our petition. This is essential for his own welfare, as well as that of the inhabitants of St. Petersburg and of Russia. Otherwise the moral bond hitherto existing between the Russian Tsar and his people may be broken. It is your duty, your great moral duty to the Tsar and the whole of the Russian people to bring this request, together with our petition herewith appended, to the notice of His Majesty the Emperor, without delay. Tell the Tsar that I and the workers, many thousands of them, putting our faith in him, have irrevocably resolved to proceed peacefully to the Winter Palace. Let him show his confidence by deeds, not in words." (The *Manchester Guardian*, January 23rd, 1905.) A further warning and protest, which also unfortunately had no effect, was issued by men of letters and of science, all of whom, including Maxim Gorky, were arrested.

to live, but not to suffer as though we were in prison or in exile.

" Our first wish was to discuss our needs with our employers, but this was refused to us : we were told that we have no legal right to discuss our conditions. We were told also that it is illegal to insist on the 8-hour working day and on the fixing of wage-rates in consultation with us. We were not allowed to discuss with the administration the behaviour of its junior staff. We asked that wages of casual labourers and women should be raised to 1 rouble a day, that overtime should be abolished and that more adequate medical attention should be provided for us so that we should not be insulted for being ill. We asked that the factories should be rebuilt so that we could work in them without suffering from draughts, rain and snow.

" All this was illegal in the opinion of our employers and of the administration. Our petition was called a criminal act and our desire to improve our working conditions an insult to them.

" Your Majesty ! We are here, many thousands of us ; we have the appearance of human beings, but in fact we have no human rights at all, not even the right to speak, to think or to meet for discussion of our requirements or the steps to be taken for the improvement of our conditions. We are turned into slaves by your officials. Anyone of us who dares to raise his voice in defence of the working class is thrown into prison, sent into exile. The mere fact of having a kind heart or a sensitive soul is regarded as a crime ; to show sympathy with the lowly, the oppressed, the tortured is also a crime. Every worker and peasant is at the mercy of your officials, who accept bribes, rob the Treasury and do not care at all for the people's interests. The bureaucracy of the government has ruined the country, involved it in a shameful war and is leading Russia nearer and nearer to utter ruin. We, the Russian workers and people, have no voice at all in the expenditure of the huge sums collected in taxes from the impoverished population. We do not even know how our money is spent. The people are deprived of any right to discuss taxes and their expenditure. The workers have no right to organise their own labour unions for the defence of their own interests.

" Is this, Your Majesty, in accordance with the laws of

God, in whose Name you reign ? How can we live under such conditions ? Is not death better—death for all of us, the workers of Russia ? And then capitalists and bureaucrats may live and enjoy themselves by robbing Russians and the Treasury. That is what we are up against, Your Majesty. And that is what has brought us to the walls of your palace. Here we have come as a last resort. Do not refuse to help your people ; liberate them from the depths of anarchy, poverty and ignorance, give them the chance to take their fate into their own hands ; take from off their shoulders the intolerable burden of bureaucracy. Destroy the barriers which divide you from your people, and let them rule the country jointly with you. Your destiny is in the happiness of your people. But this happiness is denied to us by your officials, and we live in constant sorrow and deprivation. Consider our needs calmly and without bitterness and you will see that they are for good and not for evil, both for you and for us, Your Majesty ! It is not disrespect that sends us here but the necessity of finding some way out of our intolerable situation. Russia is too great, her needs are so vast and manifold that the bureaucracy cannot rule alone. The people must be represented in the control of the country's affairs. Only the people themselves know their own needs. Command forthwith that representatives of all classes, groups, professions and trades shall come together. Let capitalists and workers, bureaucrats and priests, doctors and teachers meet together and choose their representatives. Let all be equal and free. And to this end let the election of members to the Constituent Assembly take place on general, equal, direct and secret suffrage. This is our chief request ; upon it all else depends ; this is the only cure for our great sufferings ; without it our wounds will never heal, and we shall be borne swiftly on to our death.

" But this measure alone cannot remedy all our ills. Many others are needed besides ; and these we shall put before you directly and openly, Your Majesty, as to our Father.

" These are, Your Majesty, our principal needs. Only if they are satisfied will our country be freed from slavery and misery and be led to prosperity, while the workers by means of trade unions will defend themselves from the exploitation of the capitalists and oppression at the hands of a bureaucratic government which robs the people.

" Make known your command, swear that you will satisfy our needs, and you will make Russia happy and glorious ; and your name will be stamped on our hearts and those of our descendants for ever and ever. If, however, you do not answer our prayer, we shall die here, before your palace. We have no other refuge and know no other way. There are but two ways before us, the one to freedom and happiness, the other to the grave.

" Tell us, Your Majesty, which way we are to take and we will obey ; and if it be the road of death, then may our lives be a sacrifice for long-suffering Russia. We shall not regret this sacrifice, we shall make it willingly." *

* V. Svyatlovsky, *op. cit.*, p. 389; S. N. Belousov, " History of the First Revolution of 1905." Moscow, 1924 ; *Gosizdat*, p. 68.   The following measures were also enumerated in the petition, on the introduction of which the workers insisted :—

I. Measures to counteract the ignorance and legal oppression of the Russian people :—
    1. Immediate liberation of all "political" and "religious" prisoners, as well as of all workers and peasants who have been deprived of their liberty during strikes and riots.
    2. Freedom of speech and press, of meetings and of religion.
    3. Universal and compulsory education at the expense of the State.
    4. Responsibility of Ministers before the people and a guarantee that the Administration will abide by the law.
    5. Equality before the law of all without exception.
    6. Separation of the Church from the State.

II. Measures against the poverty of the people :—
    1. Abolition of indirect taxation and introduction of progressive income tax.
    2. Abolition of redemption payments, organisation of cheap credit facilities and gradual transfer of the land to the people.
    3. Placing of orders for Army and Navy supply at home and not abroad.
    4. The cessation of the War by the will of the people.

III. Measures against the oppression of Labour by Capital :—
    1. Abolition of the existing system of factory inspection.
    2. Introduction of Boards of Conciliation and Arbitration, and of Labour Exchanges on which the workers shall be represented.   Discharge of workmen should not take place without the consent of a mixed committee.
    3. Freedom of organisation.
    4. Introduction of the eight-hour working day and regulation of overtime.

The march of an unarmed crowd on January 9th, 1905, ended in the massacre which produced a great impression, not only in Russia, but all over the world. It was, according to the writings of the eminent Russian Liberal leader, P. N. Milyukov, the greatest political outbreak Russia had ever seen. " Hundreds of victims fell dead and thousands were wounded. The movement was, however, stifled in blood. Comparative and temporary quiet was soon established. But it was evident to everybody that for the Russian Government it was a Pyrrhic victory."*

The attitude of the revolutionaries, chiefly those of the more numerous and influential Social-Democratic Party, towards the demonstration was somewhat uncertain. In their leaflets Gapon's Society was strongly criticised, but on the other hand nothing was offered in its stead, and the working masses were left without any guidance or any practical programme. " We did not take any part in the initiation of the movement and its plans. The events of January were quite unexpected by us. The strike of the Putilov workmen was a surprise for the Social Democratic Party."† There had been no attempt to dissuade the workers from joining in the demonstration. Perhaps some of the leaders of the Party hoped in their hearts for some object lesson for the workers which would teach them not to rely on the Tsar, but to take a more revolutionary line. Lenin, for instance, on receipt of the news of the massacre in St. Petersburg, wrote in the Social-Democratic

---

5. The right to strike.
6. Immediate introduction of "normal" wages (wage scales).
7. Participation of labour representatives in the preparation of a State Insurance Act.
* P. Milyukov, *op. cit.*, p. 538.
† S. Somov, " History of the Social Democratic Party," *Byloe*, 1907, Nos. 4–16, p. 22.

newspaper, *Vpered*, the official organ of the Bolshevist fraction of the Party, that " the lessons of ' Bloody Sunday ' cannot pass without some influence on the masses. Now the demand for the Constituent Assembly has to become the main slogan of all Russian workers. And the practical programme of the day must be to supply the population with arms and to organise armed revolutionary action, in order to destroy the existing ruling power and all its institutions."*

The tragedy of January 9th, 1905, had a great effect all over Russia. In Poland, the Baltic Provinces and the Caucasus, the workmen protested by calling a general strike, which soon took on the character of an insurrection and of civil war, with the industrial workmen on one side, and Government troops and armed police on the other. The latter were supported by the so-called " Black Hundreds " and *pogromshchiki*, who organised pogroms of the Jewish population and attacks on students and the intelligentsia. In the interior of Russia, the movement bore a more peaceful character, taking the form of demonstrations or of purely economic strikes.†

The strike of the railwaymen in Saratov on the Volga, on January 12th, had great influence upon the later development of events and upon the consolidation of the labour organisations themselves. It was the first successful railway strike in Russia : the Government was compelled to introduce a nine-hour working day on all its railways. From the very beginning the railwaymen elected a special bureau of delegates which, during the strike, performed the

---

* *Vpered*, No. 4, 31/18, January, 1905.
† Maurice Baring gives a vivid description of a pogrom in his story, " Pogrom," in " Half-a-minute's Silence and Other Stories." New York, 1925. See also V. Korolenko, " House No. 13 " (*Pogrom* in Kishenev).

duties of a strike committee, and its successful issue was primarily due to this. Another characteristic strike at this time was the strike in Orekhovo-Zuevo, which showed the ability of the workmen to act on their own. The workmen were confused by the revolutionary slogans, which gave no hint of a practical, positive programme, and they came to the conclusion that a demonstration, combined with economic claims, would be the best outlet for their indignation and the best way of liberating themselves from exploitation.*

The massacre of January 9th created great consternation in Government circles, and a mixed Commission, under the chairmanship of Senator Shidlovsky, was appointed. A deputation to the Tsar of thirty-four workmen was staged by the Ministry of the Interior ; it consisted mainly of nominees of the various factory administrations. The deputation, in spite of its artificial composition, took a very uncompromising attitude, and declared that they would sit on the newly-created mixed Commission of Senator Shidlovsky for the investigation of the needs of the working masses only on condition that complete freedom of speech were guaranteed there, and that the delegates were permitted to communicate and discuss the work of the Commission with their electors. They insisted also on the reopening of all branches of the labour organisations, which had been closed after the tragic Sunday. Senator Shidlovsky did not agree to these conditions, and the labour deputation refused to participate in the work of the Commission.

The deputation issued an appeal to their electors, in which they explained the motives for their refusal to collaborate with the Government representatives.

* *Cf.* D. Koltsov, *op. cit.*, Vol. II., p. 191, etc.

" We insisted on freedom of speech and the right to have free discussion as to our needs with our electors. We insisted also on the release from prison of our delegates, but this was refused, and we advised all workers to unite and insist on :

" (1) The introduction of an 8-hour day.
" (2) The appointment of labour representatives as factory inspectors.
" (3) State Insurance.
" (4) The cessation of the Japanese War.
" (5) Freedom of speech and meetings, recognition of trade unions and strikes, freedom of religion and thought and inviolability of person.
" (6) Universal education for all.
" (7) Participation of the people's representatives in the management of State affairs." *

The publication of this declaration coincided with the defeat of the Russian Army at Mukden, and it therefore appealed to the feelings of the population, who were dissatisfied with the military adventure of the Government in the Far East.

Meanwhile, the strike movement, as a protest against the policy of the Government and against economic exploitation, became a feature of everyday life. In every case the strikers acted through their representatives, and the Government authorities were obliged silently to recognise this *de facto* representation, created in the process of the strike movement. The labour representatives were not yet united in one organisation with a distinct programme ; they were for the most part " non-party " people, and their aim was to defend the common interests of all workers and peasants, to secure freedom of organisation and a democratic form of government. Later on, the slogan " Proletarians of all the world, unite,"

* *Ibid.*, Vol. II., p. 199. Mr. Afanassiev, mentioned by us on p. 64, was one of the members of the Commission.

inspired the workmen—not as a part of a definite programme, but as a general ideal.

Events after the Russian defeat by the Japanese at Mukden moved quickly. The Government became very unpopular. "The Union for Emancipation," uniting all Russian Liberals, came to the fore, and by numerous meetings and banquets paved the way for the idea of a constitutional *régime* in Russia. But the desire of the Liberals to attain their ends by peaceful evolution and strictly constitutional methods met with the stupid resistance of the old bureaucracy, which was soon swept away by the workers' political movement and the rising of peasants against their landlords.

In the summer of 1905 the whole of Russia was in a ferment. The Government did not realise the seriousness of the situation, and, through its blind resistance to the impulses of the population, provoked a wave of indignation in the autumn, of which the final outcome was the Revolution of 1905 with barricades and street-fighting.

The characteristic feature of the Russian Labour Movement at the outbreak of the Revolution was the absence of a distinct programme and of any permanent central organisations among the workers. "The contact of the working masses with the Social-Democratic Party could not give the movement any theoretical or practical unity, as the Party itself was without much unity, and, besides, its influence was purely formal and it did not penetrate to the masses of the working population."* In every case the strikers relied upon their own experience and everywhere they followed the same line, electing their delegates and entrusting to them all negotiations with the employers and Government officials.

* *Ibid*, Vol. II., p. 225.

Amongst innumerable strikes the strike of the Ivanovo-Voznessensk cotton operatives and the strike of the Moscow printers must be mentioned here. They had great influence on future events, by indicating ways and methods for the creation of labour organisations. The Ivanovo-Voznessensk strike lasted two summer months and involved 50,000 workers. The strikers created a local soviet of workers' delegates, and insisted on the convocation of a Constituent Assembly.

Ten thousand printers participated in the Moscow strike, and from the very beginning the strikers elected " the Soviet of Moscow printers' delegates," which represented the workers in 110 enterprises. The total number of delegates was 300. The Soviet held ten regular meetings, and after the strike, it passed a resolution to the effect that the delegates should become a permanent institution ; that draft rules for the future printers' union should be prepared and that the Soviet of delegates should meet again for discussion and approval of the draft.*

After these strikes the movement for the creation of labour organisations became general. The factory committees, *starostas*, delegates and "underground" unions among printers, confectioners, clerks, mechanical workers and boot-makers, etc., became the natural nuclei of trade unions (called in Russia, professional unions or simply unions).

The attitude of the Social-Democratic Party towards professional labour organisations—especially

* It must be mentioned here that there was at the same time an " underground " Printers' Union in Moscow, which was affiliated to the Social-Democratic Party, and which no doubt exercised a certain influence on the movement. (One of the pioneers of the Printers' Union was V. V. Sher, who was sentenced to ten years' imprisonment by the Soviet Government for " sabotageing the Five-Year Plan and preparing for the armed intervention of the Second International in the U.S.S.R.")

of its left wing, or Bolsheviks—was somewhat indifferent. They were afraid that the struggle for the everyday needs and purely economic demands would diminish the workers' interest in the political issue of the movement. But the need for organisation and the necessity of safeguarding economic conditions had overcome the dogma of the left-wing Social Democrats, and the formation of trade unions among the workers proceeded under the influence of the right wing, or Mensheviks, who realised that the future success of the revolution greatly depended on the existence of powerful trade unions in the country.

The newly-born trade unions, small in membership and poor in funds, naturally could not have had any marked influence on the Labour Movement during general strikes. The guidance of the Labour Movement in these revolutionary months was concentrated mainly in the hands of the St. Petersburg Soviet of Workers' Deputies, headed by a workman, I. Khrustalev-Nossar, and greatly influenced by the Social-Democratic and the Social Revolutionary Parties.*

* "The initiative of creating a Workers' Soviet of Deputies belongs to the Mensheviks," wrote B. Radin, in his book on the " First Soviet of Workers' Deputies " (St. Petersburg, 1906, p. 7), " who were always advocating the creation of a ' mass organisation.' But neither we, the Bolsheviks, nor the Mensheviks realised that the new organisation would grow tremendously, and would have such great influence."

P. Gorin, in his " History of the Soviets of Workers' Deputies in 1905 " (Moscow, 1930, p. 51), denied this statement and ascribed the authorship of this new type of organisation to the Bolsheviks. He endorsed, however, B. Radin's view by saying that " in the first days it was not clear to the Bolsheviks themselves, nor to the Mensheviks, what form would be adopted by the new organisation, the need of which was felt by all working masses."

" There has been much controversy about who first convoked the Petersburg Soviet, and whether it was the Bolsheviks or the Mensheviks ? . . . The controversy is carried on like this : one school says it was the Mensheviks ; another school says it was the Bolsheviks and the Mensheviks ; another goes so far as to affirm that it was precisely the Bolsheviks who called the Soviet. . . . But the question of who was the first to convoke the Soviet, or who was the

The creation of the Soviets of Workers' Deputies at the very outbreak of the first general strike in October 1905 is characteristic of the whole history of the Russian Labour Movement. The self-styled labour associations were all the time eager to create a central general body uniting the whole Russian working population. The outbreak of the revolutionary movement and the permanency of strikes presented such a chance, when local workers' soviets (councils) began to spring up all over the country. The initiative of the St. Petersburg, Kharkov and Moscow workers to build up an all-Russian Soviet of Workers' Deputies met therefore everywhere with whole-hearted support.

The Soviets of Workers' Deputies in their very idea, in their original structure, were nominally " non-party " organisations, but with a programme embodying all the elements of class solidarity and Socialism. In its Manifesto of October 18th, 1905, the St. Petersburg Soviet of Workers' Deputies declared that its main object was the struggle for a Constituent Assembly, for a Democratic Republic and for the introduction of the eight-hour working day in all factories and workshops as preliminary conditions of the final struggle of the proletariat for Socialism.

But in spite of this political programme, the representatives of political parties, the political unions, like the Peasants' Union and the Railway Union, were admitted to the Soviet with a consultative vote only. The anarchists were not

first to say ' Ah ! ' is a very minor question. It is not that which is important. . . . The point is not there, but that during the whole period of its activity the Petersburg Soviet had at its head a very intelligent and clever Menshevik. . . . The name of that Menshevik was Trotsky." (M. Pokrovsky, " Brief History of Russia," Vol. II., p. 320.) See also Leon Trotsky, " The History of the Russian Revolution," 3 Vols. London, 1934.

admitted at all. The newly-created trade unions held in the Soviet of Workers' Deputies only fifty-four seats, the rest of the 508 seats were kept for the deputies from factories and workshops.*

The Soviets of Workers' Deputies, which sprang up all over the country, were swept away by the reaction. They failed to rouse other classes in support of their exclusively labour programme. They were not supported by the peasants, who were in revolt against the landlords, but who held no distinct Socialist programme. They were not supported by the Russian Liberals and Democrats. But the Soviets of Workers' Deputies, in spite of their short existence, exercised great influence on the labouring masses, and gave an impetus to the consolidation of labour organisations. The first Soviets of Workers' Deputies disappeared, but the idea for which they stood was deeply rooted in the minds of workmen. Twelve years later—in 1917—it was realised on a larger scale under the name of the Soviet of Workers', Sailors', Soldiers' and Peasants' Deputies.†

* I. Khrustalev-Nossar, " The History of the Soviet of Workers' Deputies," p. 147 ; cited by P. Gorin, *op. cit.*, p. 483. There is a sad misprint in Mr. Gorin's citation : the number of trade union representatives in the Soviet was shown by him as 549, instead of 54, representing 16 trade unions.

† The Petersburg Soviet, in the opinion of M. Pokrovsky, " failed to transform itself into a *revolutionary government :* and it failed to do so because the transformation could only be effected by force of arms, and arms were not taken up before it was too late." As to the failure of the whole revolutionary movement of 1905, it was due to the fact that " the insurgent masses were not entirely revolutionary " and the Government " took advantage of the insufficiently revolutionary attitude of the masses." M. Pokrovsky, " Brief History of Russia," Vol. II., pp. 188, 239.

CHAPTER VII

THE ORIGINS OF A LEGALISED TRADE UNION MOVEMENT IN RUSSIA AND THE FIRST TRADES COUNCILS *

The Workers Factory Committees and the First Legalised Trade Unions—The Moscow Trades Council and its Activities—The St. Petersburg and other Trades Councils—Trades Councils in Germany —The London Trades Council of 1861.

THE rudimentary forms of labour organisation, created in the workers' struggle against their exploitation by employers, developed greatly, as we have seen, during the revolutionary days of 1905. The presence everywhere of delegates, chosen by the factory workers during strikes, facilitated the creation of the First Soviet of Workers' Deputies in St.

* This chapter is based on the documents and materials collected by the author in 1905–07 when he was the Honorary Secretary of the Executive Committee of the Moscow Trades Council. His investigation on this subject was approved by the University of Moscow as a thesis for a Higher Degree and published by the Seminar of Economics at the Moscow Institute of Trade and Commerce in 1913 under the title of *Moskovskoye Centralnoye Bureau Professionalnykh Soyusov* (the Moscow Trades Council), Moscow, 1913, pp. xv. + 192.

In the original publication in Russian the author gave a bibliography of sources used by him (pp. 146–150), which was composed mainly of (a) the official reports of factory inspectors ; (b) trade union journals from 1906–10 ; (c) Russian publications dealing with the trade union movement in Russia and abroad ; (d) the Protocols of the German Trades Union Conferences; (e) the works of some foreign authors, including Mr. and Mrs. Webb, Umbreit, Schmöle, I. Hüppy and others.

The references to the sources indicated in the original publication are shown in the present chapter in the footnotes. Information given without any reference to the sources is based on personal investigations of the author, and which were not available for publication at that time.

Petersburg, which devoted itself entirely to the political side of the Russian Labour Movement, whereas in Moscow the delegates from the factories and workshops concentrated their attention on the economic side of the movement and on building craft organisations in every branch of industry. Their Conference called in autumn of 1905 for the discussion of the forms of labour organisations became actually the forerunner of legalised Russian trade unionism. This conference passed at its first meeting the following resolution : "Workers of each factory should elect deputies, who should unite according to their trade (craft). These professional organisations should send their representatives to the general Soviet of Moscow workers." At its second meeting the Conference endorsed this resolution, and insisted that special "strike funds" should be formed everywhere.*

At the time of the sitting of the Conference the local "bureaux of workers' delegates" in Kharkov and other cities approached the Museum of Labour Assistance of the Imperial Russian Technical Society with a request to assist them in calling an all-Russian Congress of Labour Societies. These requests induced the Museum of Labour Assistance to convoke in Moscow a number of conferences of trade unions and various groups of workers. These joint meetings came to be known as the First Conference of Trade Unions. At this Conference was founded the Moscow Bureau of Trades Union Delegates. Its Executive was called "The Central Bureau of the Moscow Professional Unions " or the Moscow Trades Council.†

* *The Bulletins of the Museum of Labour Assistance*, Moscow, 1905. Vol. I., N1, p. 15.

† One of the first trade unions openly organised at that time in Moscow was the "Union of Workers engaged in the tea distributing 'trade" (*Soyus Chaerasvessochnikov*). Its rules were "adapted for

The Moscow Trades Council had neither written rules nor constitution at the beginning, and its membership was fixed gradually, as the need arose, by a series of resolutions. The Council admitted to its meetings outside persons and also representatives from local political organisations, but in a consultative capacity only. Voting took place, contrary to the practice of the St. Petersburg Trades Council, by unions, each union having one vote. The executive organ of the Council was an Executive Commission or Committee of " five workers," plus a representative from each of the political parties and one from the Museum of Labour Assistance.

According to calculations made by the Bureau of Trades Union Delegates, there were in Moscow at the

---

use by other trade unions, and they became the standard rules for the whole Moscow Industrial Region." (K. Dmitriev, " Trade Unions in Moscow," Moscow, 1907, p. 40.) The rules of this union will be found in the Appendix VI., p. 190. The History of the Union, written by the officials of the union, was edited in Russian by the present writer under the name: "Istoria odnogo soyus'a " ("The History of One Union "), Moscow, 1907, p. 95.

The Chairman of this union was an interesting figure. He was a workman of advanced views, and much interested in political problems, leaning in his political sympathies to the left wing of the Social-Democrats. He enjoyed great popularity amongst his fellow-workers. The liberation movement of 1905 brought him into prominence, and he might have been a good political leader if he had not had a vice which nearly cost him his life. In times of reaction he used to find an outlet for his potential energy in horse-racing. He used to gamble, and one day he lost not only his own money, but that of the union, which happened to be in his pocket. After that he disappeared from the workshop and did not come to the union. A search was made by his friends without result, and the officials of the union began to grow impatient, because, as the strike was in full swing, their position was very difficult ; they wanted to elect a new chairman. His friends, including the present writer, begged the Executive Committee to wait another fortnight, during which time vigorous attempts to find the vanished chairman ended successfully : he was found hiding in an attic, on the point of committing suicide. After much persuasion and the offer of a loan of 50 roubles to repay the union, he agreed to return. He soon regained the respect in which he was formerly held, and by his devoted work to the union lived down his past.

beginning of December 1905 some 20,000 workers organised in trade unions ; their distribution, according to the different branches of trade and industry, was as follows :

MEMBERSHIP OF TRADE UNIONS IN MOSCOW,
DECEMBER, 1905 *

Names of Unions	No. of Members.
Printers	4,000
Commercial and Industrial Employees . .	2,500
Tea-packers	2,000
Bakers	1,770
Carpenters	1,200
Tailors	1,020
Tobacco-workers	1,000
Clerks	950
Ribbon-makers	800
Workers of the Brest Railway workshops .	600
Public-house employees	500
Waiters	100
Total	16,440

It is noteworthy that the pioneers of the trade union movement in Russia were mainly the workers employed in small trades and guilds. Those engaged in big industry, like metal workers, textile workers, etc., joined the movement much later. At that time, being already partly organised politically and having delegates at nearly every factory or works, they did not feel such need of a trade union organisation.

The number of women who joined the unions at this stage was comparatively insignificant ; they looked with suspicion on trade unions ; did not see

* K. Dmitriev, " Trade Unions in Moscow," Moscow, 1907, p. 39.

much difference between them and the revolutionary organisations, and joined in greater numbers only after the legalisation of trade unions in March 1906.

One of the first tasks of the Moscow Trades Council was to draft the following Basic Principles of trade union organisation, which were approved by the Second Conference of Trade Unions :

1. The non-party character of the union ; it must not formally enter a political party.

2. A political programme must not be contained in the rules of the union, though the exchange of political opinions at the meetings of the union is desirable and admissible.

3. All unions should be proletarian in character in order to avoid " narrowly egotistical " craft organisation.

4. Each union must strive to unite all workers of a given trade throughout Russia.

5. Each union must be " fighting " in character ; financial assistance to members must be given sparingly and only temporarily.

6. All unions must preserve their proletarian character ; mixed unions of employers and workers are inadmissible ; joint unions of high- and low-paid workers are undesirable.

7. Unions embracing whole branches of industry are to be preferred to those built on a narrow craft basis.

8. The principle of democracy within the union must be developed to the utmost ; the drawing in of the greatest possible numbers of members into the activities of the union is very desirable (soviets of delegates) ; meetings of members must be held as frequently as possible.

9. The educational activities in the union (libraries, clubs, meetings) must be encouraged.

10. The local unification of the unions in the form of trades councils must not impair the full autonomy of individual unions.*

These Basic Principles of trade union organisation reflected to a certain extent some of the main principles of the European trade unions. We find, for instance, a similarity in the recommendation to form "unions embracing whole branches of industry," instead of craft unions (§ 7).

The relations between the unions and their trades councils were also outlined, differing little from the practice of English trades councils or German *Gewerkshaftskartelle* : the trades councils must not impair the full autonomy of the individual unions (§ 10).

The recommendation to form non-Party unions did not exclude the possibility of influence of political parties on trade unions ; on the contrary, it was considered advisable and desirable to hold meetings for the discussion of political problems (§ 2). The underlying idea of this recommendation was that the unions must not have any formal connection with or affiliation to the political parties ; it would, otherwise, split the unity of the trade union movement and would endanger the very existence of trade unions owing to the illegal position of all Socialist Parties in Russia.†

There were some dissimilarities in methods and functions. The authors of the Basic Principles, for instance, not only endorsed the " war theory, based on the philosophy of the class struggle," but went

* The verbatim Report of the Second Conference of Trade Unions. St. Petersburg, 1906, p. 47.

† There was not much disagreement at that time on the question of " neutrality " of trade unions amongst the Russian Social-Democrats. Lenin himself shared this view up to 1908. See V. Dokukin, " Bolshevism and Menshevism in the Trade Union Movement, Leningrad, 1926," p. 43.

much further, saying that the trade unions ought to have a " proletarian," " fighting," militant character. The belief in strikes as the only method of struggle and a last resource was now adopted as the most important of methods to be used by the trade unions.*

They were opposed, further, not only to the " mixed unions of employers and workers," but to " joint unions of high and low paid workers " (§ 6). They rejected the principle of friendly benefits : " financial assistance to members must be given sparingly and only temporarily " (§ 5).

The Basic Principles laid great stress on the " drawing in of the greatest possible number of members into the activities of the union (soviets of delegates) " and to the meetings of members (§ 8). The soviets of delegates were considered to be the soul of every union, a kind of labour parliament, similar to the " Parliament of Cottonspinners," described by Mr. and Mrs. Webb in their book on Industrial Democracy.†

The main task of every trade union was to attract as many people as possible to the general meetings and to the activities of the unions. The payment of membership fees was considered to be of secondary importance. It was quite sufficient for everyone to become a member of the union by entering (" registering ") his name in the list of members at the trade union office. In the early days of formation of trade unions, the non-payment of fees did not deprive the member *of voting or participation* in any of the activities of the union.‡

* *Cf.* C. M. Lloyd, " Trade Unionism." London, Ed. 1921, p. 77.
† S P., " The Soviets of Delegates " in " The History of One Union," Moscow, 1907, p. 29 ; K. Dmitriev, " The Trade Union Organisation " in " Help Worker," Moscow, 1907, p. 19.
‡ The membership of trade unions varied greatly in Russia from month to month. The exodus of " registered " members was always

This was one of the weak points of the practice of Russian trade unions. They disregarded the need for an accumulation of funds. This failure to pay attention to finance led to disastrous results during the later stage of the development of trade unions. They lacked security and stability, and it was easy for employers' associations to break them up. Absence of funds made it impossible for them to render any substantial help and relief to their unemployed members ; social insurance was left entirely to the discretion of employers, and the trade unions had no word to say about it.

The authority of the Moscow Trades Council, in spite of this, grew every day. The workers consulted the Council on many points, which they had formerly put to the factory inspectors * All groups of unorganised workmen and professional men were seeking the assistance of the Council. The desire to form unions was so popular at that time that there

very great in times of police reprisals and during industrial depressions. The Union of Carpenters and Joiners, for instance, gives the following figures :

1907	No. of " Registered " Members	No. of those who paid their Fees	Per cent.
July	509	458	90
August . . .	748	387	51·7
September .	862	527	61·1
October . .	991	489	49·3
November . .	1,060	407	39·1
December . .	1,092	275	25·2

(S. Ainsaft, " The History of the Union of Carpenters and Joiners." Moscow, 1928, p. 139.)

* " In January almost everyone applied to the factory inspector. From October 1905 onwards the ' class-conscious ' workers turned down the employers' proposals to call in the inspector and only the ' non class-conscious ' continued to apply to him. During December there is to be observed a complete absence of applications to the inspectors since the whole movement was led by the ' class-conscious ' workers." (Typewritten Reports of Factory Inspectors.)

was hardly a profession or trade where such an attempt was not made. The present writer recalls the following rather curious case. Living in an isolated and lonely street on the outskirts of Moscow, he saw one day in front of his window some people busily engaged in removing old sleepers from the railway line and throwing them over the wooden fence. On the other side of the fence a horse and cart were waiting, and another lot of people were loading it with the sleepers. To the occasional passer-by in this lonely neighbourhood it would have seemed that nothing was wrong, and that the workmen on the railway were simply doing their job. But it was not so. Having noticed that I was watching them, they stopped their work, came to my window and addressed me very politely : " We hope you do not mind our doing this. We know you. We heard you speaking at the People's House. It is very good of you to help working-people to organise their own unions. Perhaps you will help us also to organise one." After receiving from me elementary information on how to organise a union, they went away and greeted me cheerfully from the cart full of sleepers. In a few days' time I received a written request, addressed to the " Speaker at the People's House," to come to a general meeting to explain the idea of a union and how to organise one. The application was signed : " Committee of the Krestovsky pickpockets."*

After the general strike in December 1905 all trade unions had to face very trying conditions. It was impossible for the unions to hold meetings openly, and the union executives themselves managed to meet only under great difficulty. The majority of the unions went completely to pieces, and those which survived had but a handful of members. Extreme depression

* The *Krestovsky zastava* is one of the Moscow suburbs.

was widespread among the working population, and to many, joining a trade union seemed nothing but political action against the existing *régime*.

At the beginning of 1906 the Executive Commission of the Moscow Trades Council made an attempt to re-establish the Council and to estimate the resources of the surviving unions. It was found that the unions gradually began to recover, but that the position of trade unions remained highly ambiguous. Although they were not interfered with by the police so long as they concerned themselves only with peaceful economic activities, they were still " not permitted " by law.

The undefined position of the unions and the resulting legal confusion was admitted by the Government itself. Thus, during the discussion of the proposed trade union law by the State Council, Count Witte, the Secretary of State, pointed out that " the struggle of capital and labour is inevitable under present conditions of industrial production, and the task of the legislator lies not in opposing it, but only in giving it legal expression. Unions organised among both workers and employers can serve as the best means of securing this."

And in the middle of February 1906 the " Temporary Rules Concerning Societies and Unions " were published by the Government, which became law on March 4th, 1906.*

At first the unions regarded this law with great suspicion, and were faced with the problem of whether they should legalise their position by registering their rules, or whether they should continue as before a *de facto* existence. The untenability of the latter policy soon became obvious, as the non-

---

* V. Svyatlovsky " The Trade Union Movement in Russia." St. Petersburg, 1907, p. 353.

registered unions continually suffered from the repressive actions of the police.

The Moscow Trades Council saw no reason why the unions should not submit their rules to registration, and it therefore adopted the following resolution : " The Moscow Trades Council while recognising that the Temporary Rules concerning Societies and Unions by no means guarantee that freedom which is necessary for trade union activity but on the contrary aim at stifling the trade union movement . . . nevertheless believes that unions can make use of the Temporary Rules for the development of the proletarian struggle, and that, while in no way altering their character and the direction of their activities, they should register their names in conformity with the second section of the Rules of 4th March."*

While energetically advising registration, however, the Trades Council could not adopt this course itself, since the Temporary Rules excluded this possibility by laying it down that " the combination of two or more trade unions to form a single union is prohibited." The Moscow Trades Council continued to exist on a semi-legal basis, which, however, did it little harm except by making necessary a certain amount of discretion and " underground " work.

The convocation of the First Duma caused increased trade union activity ; the trade unions frequently sent addresses to the Duma. General meetings of trade union members began to be more largely attended, and at the same time it was becoming more and more apparent to everyone that the position of the Duma was very insecure, since the intention of the Government to take decisive action was obvious. It was not long, in fact, before the

* The " Russkoe Slovo." Moscow, 1906, No. 79.

First Duma was dissolved, and repressive action against trade unions was renewed.*

On the day of the dissolution of the First Duma an Extraordinary and unusually well-attended meeting of the Trades Council was held, at which delegates from many organisations which had not previously taken part were present. At the same time meetings of union Executives and of workers' delegates took place everywhere : the question of immediate action was hurriedly and vehemently discussed. The local political organisations did not come to any decision, but waited for a lead from the Trades Council. This shows how great was the authority of the latter among the Moscow workers. At the Extraordinary Meeting of the Moscow trade unions the majority voted for a policy of " wait and see." This policy naturally disappointed the left wing of the Social-Democratic Party, who were in favour of " direct " action.

Not long after the dissolution of the Duma, when the first impressions of the repressive measures had to some extent passed away and when the surviving unions had managed to adapt themselves to the new conditions, the absence of connecting links between the unions became more and more inconvenient. It was felt necessary to widen the limits of their activities, to enliven the work of the unions by means of lectures and reports, to put in order the internal organisation of the unions, and finally to establish some measure of unity with regard to a number of basic questions of policy. The following new Rules of the Moscow Trades Council were adopted :

RULES OF THE MOSCOW TRADES COUNCIL.

1. The Moscow Trades Council renders assistance to trade unions and unifies their activities ; with this object

* The First Duma was convoked in May, 1906, and dissolved in July of the same year.

it collects statistical data and reports concerning the activities of trade unions, discusses general principles of the trade union movement, issues the necessary literature, organises libraries, clubs, lectures, etc., and assumes the initiative in calling conferences and meetings.

2. The Trades Council is an advisory institution for the trade unions.

3. The Trades Council is a non-party organisation and, in order to secure co-ordinated action, enters into relations with the different proletarian parties and organisations, inviting to its meetings representatives of the political organisations and sending its representatives to non-party proletarian organisations (for example, to the Unemployed Committee).

The Trades Council retains the right in certain cases to make in its own name declarations to various organisations and institutions and to delegate representatives to these.

The Structure of the Moscow Trades Council

1. The right to send representatives to the Trades Council is enjoyed by all unions possessing some kind of organisation, such as a proper Union Executive or merely a Delegates' meeting.

2. The unions send to the Trades Council representatives elected by either the Executive of the Union or by a Delegates' meeting, or by the General Meeting of all members of the union. (The last method is the most desirable.)

3. Each union has the right, regardless of the size of its membership, to send to the Trades Council *two representatives with full voting rights*. (Unions are recommended to elect candidates who could at any time replace a representative in the event of his leaving the Trades Council.)

4. The right of representation on the Trades Council can be enjoyed by those institutions and organisations which carry on work among the proletariat and assist the growth of the trade union movement. At the same time, in each individual case the right of granting representation rests with the Trades Council.

5. The Trades Council elects from among its members an Executive Commission to carry out its decisions : it possesses the right of co-opting persons necessary and useful to it, without granting them voting rights.*

* " The Report of the Moscow Trades Council, 1906." No. 4.

In accordance with the new Rules, the Moscow Trades Council formed an Executive Commission which consisted again of five members ; representatives of the political organisations were also admitted, but only in an advisory capacity. Meetings of the Executive Commission were always most businesslike, and were regarded with respect by the unions. Apart from the Executive Commission, during the four or five months of its intensive activity at the end of 1906, the Moscow Trades Council created a number of other bodies, of which the most important were the Legal and Medical Commissions.

The Legal Commission was formed because the daily presence of the Secretary at the office of the Trades Council attracted many inquiries from workers, some of which had no relation to trade union matters. He was approached for advice as to the best way of settling a grievance against an employer, and asked to decide whether it was worth while lodging a complaint with the factory inspector, etc. Advice was frequently sought with regard to divorces and other matters relating to the Civil Code. Even peasants applied for advice on disputes over land.

Just as numerous were the applications to the Council for the advice of a " good but cheap doctor," and frequent complaints of the " negligent attitude " of the hospitals towards the workers, and this induced the Trades Council to make arrangements for medical assistance also. But it succeeded only in getting a number of private doctors to serve the most important unions and to secure a reduction of up to 50 per cent. in the charges of certain chemist shops and hospitals. It was later found possible to organise medical assistance on a fairly large scale by splitting up Moscow into ten or fifteen districts with ninety-four doctors treating union members. But this organisation did not last long.

The next body set up by the Trades Council was the Lecturers' or Propagandist Group. The necessity for unifying the propaganda and educational work in the unions had been apparent ever since the formation of the Trades Council ; but the task was a very complicated one, because there were great differences of political outlook. The struggle for influence and control in the unions sometimes took an extreme form. Thus, in some unions where there were a number of conflicting and equally well-represented political beliefs among the members, the Executives of the Unions worked out before each general meeting a set of rules controlling not only the number of speakers to be allotted to each party, but also, within certain limits, the contents of their speeches, so as to reduce as much as possible opportunities for conflicts of opinion. Under these circumstances, the creation of any sort of uniform body was obviously extremely difficult, and the Council decided that the Propagandist Group should be composed only of persons who " adhered to the proletarian class point of view and recognised the Rules of the Trades Council."

The Moscow Trades Council had no printed journal, and issued its resolutions in the form of separate leaflets and pamphlets. But the absence of a journal was offset by the existence in Moscow of two weekly papers, *Nashe Dielo* (Our Affairs) and *Rabochy Soyus* (The Workers' Union), which willingly printed all that was most interesting and relevant in the trade union movement.

The whole apparatus of the Trades Council suffered greatly from lack of funds. Public subscription produced only 63 roubles 83 kopeks. The monthly subscriptions of trade unions were paid irregularly.

The ready cash of the Trades Council up to the moment when it took over the funds of the Soviet of Workers' Deputies never exceeded some 200 roubles.

According to information collected by the Trades Council, there were in the autumn of 1906, 29,700 " registered " members of trade unions in Moscow.* Their distribution according to the different branches of trade and industry was as follows :

MEMBERSHIP OF TRADE UNIONS IN MOSCOW,
SEPTEMBER, 1906

Names of Unions	No. of " Registered " Members
Printers	8,000
Metal workers	4,500
Tailors	3,000
Confectioners	1,500
Clerks and accountants	1,500
Tobacco workers	1,300
Tea packers	1,200
Plumbers	1,200
Builders	1,100
Carpenters and joiners	1,000
Commercial and industrial employees . .	900
White metal workers	700
Textiles	600
Employees in chemist shops	500
Cooks	500
Technicians	400
Grocers' assistants	400
Ribbon-makers	300
Leather workers	300
Assistants in butchers' shops . . .	200
Domestic servants	200
Bootmakers	200
Photographers	100
Dispensers in chemist shops	100
	29,700

* The *Labour Union*, Moscow, 1906, No. 4, p. 7 : and the *Nashe Dielo*, Moscow, 1906, No. 4, p. 9.

Among the activities of the Moscow Trades Council must be mentioned here its endeavours to build larger unions, embracing a whole profession or industry. It was planned to convene a conference of trade unions from the provinces, with which the Moscow Trades Council was in touch.*

The strike movement also took up a great deal of the Trades Council's time and energy, and the unions were very glad of its support. Strikes were mostly called with the knowledge of the Trades Council, and even the largest unions considered it their duty to bring proposed strikes to the notice of the Trades Council.

Among the strikes of this period must be mentioned those at certain engineering works, and the widespread movement among tailors. In connection with the tailors' strike, the Trades Council issued the following appeal :

" In view of the immense significance of the tailors' strike (at the firm of Mandel and Co.) not only for the tailors' union but also for all Moscow unions ; furthermore, in view of the fact that the Conference of all owners of large-scale tailoring establishments in Moscow has decided to declare a lock-out, the Trades Council is unanimously in favour of the most energetic participation in the struggle of the Tailors' Union against the Union of Owners of Tailoring establishments.

" With this end in view, the Trades Council decided : first, to discuss the tailors' strike at all executive and delegate meetings and to collect money for the strikers ; second, to issue in the name of the Trades Council a leaflet to all workers calling them to support the strikers, and, moreover, to urge all consumers to boycott all tailoring establishments where workers are on strike and

* The unions from the following towns were expected to be represented at the Conference : Moscow, Serpukhov, Kolomna, Bogorodsk, Orekhovo-Zuevo, Ivanovo-Voznessensk, Shuya, Kostroma, Kineshma, Yaroslavl, Rybinsk, Tver, Kaluga, Tula, Smolensk, Ryazan, Oreol, Vyazniki and others.

where a lockout has been declared ; third, to issue a leaflet to the strikers ; fourth, to discuss in the Trade Union press the significance of the present strike for all the workers of Moscow." *

The unions warmly responded to the appeal, and in a short time 600 roubles were collected.

One of the most serious problems for the Trades Council and for all the unions at that time was the question of unemployment. The Trades Council had not, so far, taken any direct part in the organisation of the unemployed, which had been dealt with by a special Unemployed Council (Soviet), by the Moscow Town Council, and to some extent by the Imperial Russian Technical Society. After the dissolution of the Unemployed Council the Moscow Trades Council decided to organise the unemployed through the unions and to create a United Commission of Unemployed connected with the Trades Council, and subordinated to it. Its duties were to open new " eating-rooms " and to maintain those already in existence. The funds of the United Commission were to be supplied by a contribution from the unions for every unemployed worker receiving meals or other assistance from the Commission. But we must admit that the experiments of the United Commission of Unemployed were not very successful.

When those unemployed for whom the unions had paid contributions had been given meals, the Commission spent the rest of the money on supplying meals to others, but, in view of the great demand, it was unable to satisfy everyone, and this resulted in increasing dissatisfaction. Complaints were also made that the eating-rooms fed only a chosen few, and discontent was still further increased by certain abuses in the management of the rooms. As time

* The *Labour Union*, Moscow, 1906, No. 3, p. 7.

went on, the conditions became worse and worse, and the most powerful unions declared their intention of making separate provision in future for their unemployed members. In the face of such an attitude of the unions themselves, it was obvious that the eating-rooms could not last long, and after a short time they closed down completely. Thus ended the attempt to organise the unemployed through the United Commission of Trade Unions.*

The political life of the country naturally exercised

---

* According to the Reports of the United Commission (published in the *Labour Union*, 1906, Nos. 3, 4, 5), its income and expenditure account was as follows :

INCOME AND EXPENDITURE ACCOUNT OF THE UNITED COMMISSION OF UNEMPLOYED, SEPTEMBER–NOVEMBER 1906

Income

	roubles	kop.
By the former Council of Unemployed . . .	833	—
„ „ Commercial and Industrial Employees' Union	176	34
„ „ Metal Workers' Union	285	—
„ „ Printers' Union	91	63
„ „ Bakers' Union	72	—
„ „ Clerks' and Accountants' Union . . .	52	85
„ „ Confectioners' Union	50	—
„ „ Union of Postal and Telegraph Employees .	55	—
„ „ Engineers' Union	30	—
„ „ Plumbers' Union	20	—
„ „ Workers of the Sokolnichesky Park, the Moscow Municipality, Unions of Tailors, Weavers and Tobacco Workers . . .	49	35
„ Voluntary Subscriptions	8	—
„ Various Unions (details not given in the Report)	345	—
	2,068	17

Expenditure

	roubles	kop.
To the Sretenskaya Eating-room	689	78
„ „ Butyrskaya „	655	—
„ „ Rogozhskaya „	241	—
„ Loans	25	—
„ Petty Cash	20	—
„ Eating-rooms (no details given) . . .	165	—
	1,795	78
Balance	272	39
	2,068	17

a great influence on the trade unions, and in spite of their being mainly occupied with the strike movement and organisational work, they reacted acutely to all the important social and political events of the period. Even the Trades Council, overburdened as it was with a mass of routine work, was in the habit of coming forward with its opinion on this or that topic of the day, trying always to take a non-party attitude.

The following incident is very characteristic in this respect. It was announced that certain members of the British Parliament intended to visit Russia. The Government and all political parties were preparing to receive the guests and were planning a ceremonial reception for them. The Trades Council, not wishing to force its opinion upon the unions, suggested that they should discuss the question at their executive and delegate meetings, and intended to defer its decision till after they had done so. Meanwhile the Government, acting through diplomatic channels, had turned down the proposed visit, and the Constitutional Democratic Party (*Cadets*) decided to send an address of welcome to England, at the same time circulating it widely among the public and workmen.

The Trades Council advised the unions not to sign the address, and elected a special Commission to compose a separate one from the trade unions. Such an address was drawn up, but no signatures were collected for it, as by that time the general feeling had changed, and the whole matter had been forgotten in the flood of other important events.*

The next question over which the divergent political opinions of the members of the Moscow Trades Council came into conflict was that of the

* This reminds us of the arrangements made by the London Trades Council in 1862 to welcome Garibaldi to England and in 1864 to welcome a deputation of French workmen arriving in England.

"Workers' Congress." At that time this question was discussed everywhere, and a very considerable literature grew up around it. But it never got beyond the discussion stage. A special meeting of the Trades Council was devoted to it, but in view of the divergence of opinion shown in the discussion, the question had to be left open.

An accession of funds from the Soviet of Workers' Deputies to the amount of over 2,000 roubles exercised an invigorating influence on the activities of the Trades Council. The trade unions began to pay more attention to it. Fewer strikes were called without the Trades Council's sanction, since many unions were interested in securing its agreement to a proposed strike and its financial assistance. The success of the strike movement in Moscow at that time was to a certain extent due to this accession of the Soviet of Workers' Deputies funds.*

* The expenditure of the Moscow Trades Council from the funds of the Soviet of Workers' Deputies during January–May 1907 was as follows :

SUBSIDIES, LOANS, ETC.

	Roubles
To the Commercial and Industrial Employees' Union .	100
,, ,, Union of Postal and Telegraph Employees . .	100
,, ,, Union of Floor-polishers	20
,, ,, Union of Shoemakers	80
,, ,, Union of Textile Workers	200
,, ,, Union of Upholsterers	200
,, ,, Workers of the K. Factory	50
,, ,, Return of sums borrowed	90
,, ,, Lodz Lock-out Fund	300
,, ,, Vitebsk Leather workers	30
To sending delegates into the provinces to prepare for the Trade Unions Conference	150
,, sending the Secretary to St. Petersburg . . .	50
,, sending a special delegate to St. Petersburg . .	100
,, the Secretariat of the Trades Council . . .	250
,, Eating-rooms for the unemployed	100
,, editing the Journal	200
,, Propaganda Fund	150
	2,170

(S. P. Turin, " The Moscow Trades Council." Moscow, 1913, pp. 99–100.)

In almost all the important industrial centres of Russia where there were trade unions more or less well established, there existed trades councils. In some places they were called " The Bureau of Delegates," in others "The Central Bureau," " The League of Assistance to the Trade Union Movement " (Kursk, Nizhni-Novgorod), " The Council of Trade Union Deputies " (Tiflis), etc. However, in spite of these differences in title, all the trades councils had one common feature : the desire to unify the local unions and to encourage workers, mainly those engaged in small crafts and guilds, to set up trade union organisations. " Organisation and Propaganda " was their motto throughout the whole of Russia.

The best organised trades councils were those of Moscow and St. Petersburg. The others followed their guidance.

The Rules of the Moscow and St. Petersburg Trades Councils were typical of the rest. Especially important were the clauses defining the relationship of the Council to the trade unions of which it was composed. Both the St. Petersburg and the Moscow Trades Councils recognised that the trades council was merely a guiding body, and " could not take any decisions which should be binding on the unions which it united." The same was the case in other towns, with the exception of Simferopol, where the trades council considered that its decisions should be binding on the smaller unions.

The history of the development of the Russian trades councils recalls in many respects that of the German and English trades councils. In Germany, organisations similar to trades councils, called *Gewerkschaftskartelle*, were originally also set up without any constitution ; their primary task was to guide the strike movement, to organise the collection of money and to distribute it according to their discretion. As the "central" unions developed, they came into conflict with the trades councils, and this state of affairs induced the Cologne Congress of Trade Unions to prepare Rules for the *Gewerkschaftskartelle* and to define their tasks more clearly, especially with regard to the strike movement and the collection of funds to help strikers. The *Gewerkschaftskartelle*, according to these Rules, did not possess the right to make collections without the consent of the General Trade Union Commission, which was the highest authority in the German trade union movement.

In the first paragraph of the Rules, passed by the Cologne Congress, the *Gewerkschaftskartell* was defined as an organisation of trade union delegates, representing economic and social-political interests of the workers. Its membership was fixed by the second paragraph of the Rules, as follows : one delegate from each trade union having less than 200 members, two delegates from each trade union having 200 to 500 members ; for big unions, one delegate for each 500 members.*

A tendency to limit the power of the *Gewerkschaftskartell* had also been shown at the Frankfurt Congress in 1899, where a resolution was adopted outlining its tasks. In this it was stated that it must deal with local interests of general trade union importance, that is, find work for the unemployed (*Arbeitsnachweis*), provide the unemployed with lodgings (*Herbergswesen*), collect and work up statistical material, set up libraries, secretariats, etc., defend the workers' interests in dealings with the management, and organise joint action during the elections for insurance offices and industrial courts.

* " Jahresbericht des Gewerkschaftskartells." Dresden, 1908, p. 157.

Further, jointly with other organisations, the *Gewerk-schaftskartell* must assist propaganda in those trades which were not in a position to carry this on properly themselves.

The *Gewerkschaftskartelle* were also bound to prepare reports on local conditions of labour and the relative strength of labour and capital for the unions intending to declare a strike. Financial support of a strike on the part of the *Gewerkschaftskartelle* could be permitted only with the consent of the central organisation of the union concerned in the strike. Questions of negotiations concerning wages, etc., arising in any trade, were to be decided independently by the union in question.*

The German *Gewerkschaftskartelle* did not have the right to ask the local branches of the central unions to send their representatives to their meetings. The Cologne Congress, though, advised the unions' executives to urge their branches to join the *Gewerk-schaftskartelle*. This absence of the right to ask for representatives to be sent to their meetings is characteristic also of the Russian trades councils.

Another question that arises in comparing the Rules of the Russian Trades Councils and that of the German *Gewerkschaftskartelle* is the method of representation of the unions on the trades council. The Rules of both the Moscow and the St. Petersburg Councils provided for the admission of an equal number of representatives from each union. Proportional representation did not exist and decisions were usually arrived at by a majority of votes. Occasionally, however, controversial or especially important questions were first referred to the executives of the unions for preliminary discussion.

* *Cf.* " Protokoll der Verhandl. des dritten Kongresses der Gewerkshaften Deutschlands." Frankfurt a/M., 1899, pp. 214–15.

(For example, in Moscow, the question of the transfer of funds from the Soviet of Workers' Deputies to the Trades Council, the question of political action after the dissolution of the First Duma, etc., were so discussed.) The rules of the German *Gewerkschaftskartelle* provided for proportional representation ; unions with a membership of up to 200 elected one delegate, those with from 200 upwards elected two. Large unions sent one delegate for every 500 members. If a union had branches, delegates were not sent from each branch, but the total number of members in all branches was taken as the basis for the election of delegates.

It is certain that the principle of proportional representation would have been accepted in Russia also, if the unions had been larger and better developed and if the trades councils themselves had been established on a sufficiently firm basis. Under existing circumstances, however, the principle of proportional representation might even have proved harmful, as it would have lessened the importance of the small unions which needed the assistance of a trades council far more than the stronger ones.

There was also a similarity between the Russian trades councils and the English ones. In the Rules of the London Trades Council of May 7th, 1861, we find, for instance, the following definition of its aims :

" 8. That the duties of the Council shall be to watch over the general interests of labour, political and social, both in and out of Parliament ; and to use its influence to support any measure likely to benefit trade unions ; also, to publish if necessary an Annual Trades Union Directory.

" 9. The Council to have power to investigate cases of appeal made to them by trades in distress. If, after strict investigation, they are found worthy of support, the Council shall recommend them to other trades for assistance. The Council to have the power to furnish deputations on application with credentials to the trades of London ; but in no case shall the Council have power to make levies for any purpose."*

The existence of trades councils, especially of those in Moscow and St. Petersburg and in the South of Russia, was on the whole very useful. They helped to secure more thorough trade union organisation and encouraged the workers to organise. Without the assistance of trades councils the development of the Russian trade union movement would have been much slower ; and in the absence of a unifying body the unions might not have obtained that relative unity in organisation which characterised the early history of the Russian trade union movement.

* Cicely Rhodes, " A History of the Trades Council, 1860–75." London, 1920, pp. 12–13.

CHAPTER VIII

THE GROWTH OF REACTION

The Reaction after the 1905 Revolution—The Attitude of the Police towards Trade Unions—Employers' Organisations—A new Method in Strikes—The Strike of Textile Workers—Trade Unions, their Membership, Organisation and Functions—The Dissolution of the Duma and its Effect on the Labour Movement—The Labour Press.

Soon after the Revolution of 1905 the Tsarist Government, though limited to a certain extent by the Duma, made a firm bid to regain its prestige among the population and to grasp once more the control of State affairs. The liberties won by the Revolution were recaptured by the Government step by step. Political reaction grew steadily, and everywhere there were signs of approaching industrial crisis and trade depression. All this affected labour conditions in the first instance : unemployment increased, and the strike movement lost momentum, owing to supervision and interference by the police ; the existing trade unions were now faced with the constant menace of being closed down for the slightest offence against the regulations and rules concerning registration.*

At the same time the creation of powerful em-

* In a circular letter of the Police Department on May 10th, 1907, it was laid down as follows : " It is necessary to pay very serious attention to the activities and membership of trade unions. Their registration should be allowed only after they have shown that they have no connection at all with the Social-Democratic groups. Trade unions must be shut down at once if their activities go beyond the regulations prescribed by law." N. Vanag and S. Tomsinsky, " Economic Development of Russia." Moscow, *Gosizdat*, 1928, Vol. II., p. 54.

ployers' organisations, mainly in the metal, textile and other branches of industry, was driving the trade unions to adopt a new method in strikes. It was no use calling a strike in any factory or firm ; it would be smashed immediately like a fishing-boat by heavy seas. The new method consisted in endeavours to convert the collective or " group " strikes, which embraced several factories in the same branch of industry, into general strikes in every branch of industry. One of the first strikes of this new type was called on July 2nd, 1907, by the Second Conference of Delegates of the textile workers in the Moscow Industrial Province. This strike was defeated by the employers' organisation, but it gave an impetus to other unions to follow the same path.*

* This strike was called for the following reasons :
   1. The existence of appalling conditions of work in textile factories in the Moscow district.
   2. The great rise in prices of necessities and comparatively very slight increase in wages.
   3. Very high profits made by employers owing to the flourishing condition of the textile trade.
   4. The creation of a powerful employers' organisation dictating conditions of work for the whole industry.
   5. The failure of individual strikes during 1905–1906 in Ivanovo-Voznessensk, Kostroma and other places.
The strikers were advised by the Conference to insist on the following conditions of work :
   1. The introduction of an eight-hour working day.
   2. Continuous rest during the week-end of not less than forty-two hours.
   3. Abolition of overtime and of night work.
   4. Prohibition of the employment of women and children in industries and workshops dangerous to their health.
   5. An annual month's holiday with full pay.
   6. Increase of wages and the introduction of a minimum wage.
   7. Freedom of trade union organisations ; introduction of arbitration courts and of collective agreements.
   8. The employment of workers through their trade union as well as their discharge with the union's consent.

(M. Balabanov, " From 1905 to 1917." Moscow, *Gosizdat*, 1927, p. 82.)

The necessity of strengthening trade union organisation and the need for collective action in each branch of industry covering a whole district or region was also very pressing, and the unions were busily engaged in the creation of unions on a larger scale, uniting the workers in each profession or branch of industry not only in one locality or town, but in the whole of an industrial district. Some of the industrial workers had already set up all-Russian unions : these were the workers in the tea-distributing trade, tailors, workers in the building industry, metal workers and clerks in wholesale and retail trade. Others were engaged in building their regional organisations in the Moscow Industrial Province (comprising ten *gubernias* adjacent to Moscow), in the Donets Basin, in the Volga Province, and in the Crimea. A third type of amalgamation was to be found in unions built on the principle of nationality : Polish, Jewish, etc. The majority of the last named were closely connected with the Socialist or Social-Democratic organisations, whereas the all-Russian and regional unions were based on the principle of " neutrality," with a distinct " class " character.

The trades councils also tried to convene conferences of all trade unions, as well as an all-Russian Trade Union Congress ; but their attempts met with only partial success. The first conference in the autumn of 1905 and the second in March 1906 were not truly representative, and their main work consisted in adopting model rules, which were of great help to the trade unions. The third conference did not take place till February 1917, and the first all-Russian Congress took place in 1918, on January 7th.*

* The membership of trade unions in 1907 and their distribution, according to different branches of industry, was as follows :

At the same time the trade unions did not neglect their other functions. Every union was very much concerned with the problem of relief of its own unemployed, and several big trade unions set up various commissions for working out schemes of collective bargaining and social insurance. But the realisation of these schemes was made difficult by the insecure legal status of the unions and the absence of funds.

Usually more than a half of all trade unions' funds were spent on strikes, administration, and educational activities. The following balance-sheet of the Metal-Workers' Union may be considered as typical for all

MEMBERSHIP OF TRADE UNIONS IN 1907 (a)

Industry	No. of Unions	Membership
1. Coal-mining	5	2,475
2. Carpentry	38	9,927
3. Leather	85	12,066
4. Metal	81	54,173
5. Tailoring	59	14,322
6. Printing	72	28,654
7. Food	78	24,848
8. Building.	43	12,396
9. Textile	25	37,214
10. Shop Assistants and Clerks . .	101	32,475
11. Other	65	17,005
Total	652	245,555

In Moscow alone there were 46 unions with 48,051 members, and in the Moscow Province (including Moscow), 90 unions with 60,942 members. In St. Petersburg there were 44 unions with 51,782 members, and in the Petersburg Province (including St. Petersburg), 61 unions with 53,514 members Next to these two main industrial areas was Poland with 62 unions and 47,712 members. More than a half of all trade union members, according to the above figures, were recruited from these three provinces, while in the rest of Russia about 100,000 workers were organised in unions.

(a) D. Grinevich, " The Trade Union Movement in Russia," p. 285.

big trade unions ; the funds of the small unions lasted only till the first strike, which immediately swallowed the whole of their monies.

INCOME AND EXPENDITURE OF THE ST. PETERSBURG METAL-WORKERS' UNION, 1908. (*In Roubles*)

Income		Expenditure	
Membership fees . . 18,818		Administration . . 4,113	
Subscription for the		Cultural-educational	
Journal . . . 1,110		activities . . . 2,431	
Donations . . . 5,105		Strikes . . . 4,960	
Other 964		Subsidies (benefits) . 1,067	
		Other 604	
25,997			13,175
		Balance . . 12,822	
25,997			25,997

Donations according to this table amounted to one-fifth of the total income. Administration cost 31·3 per cent., strikes 40 per cent., and cultural activities 18·3 per cent. of the total expenditure.*

The size of the Russian trade unions was another obstacle to the development of a general scheme of social insurance or of a system of benefits on the pattern of the European trade unions. The majority of trade unions were very small in size : 349 unions out of a total number of about 600 unions had less than 100 members each ; over 100 unions counted their membership from 100 to 200 people in each union. The number of trade unions with over 2,000 members was only twenty-two. The majority therefore, could not deal adequately with their unemployed members, and only the strongest unions managed to pay out travelling expenses during the strike, and to give unemployment benefit for a short

* "Materials relating to the economic conditions and organisation of Metalworkers in Petrograd." Petersburg, 1909, Appendix, pp. 8–16.

time : preference was given always to those who lost their jobs because of a strike.*

The dissolution of the Second Duma on June 3rd, 1907, made the existence of labour organisations more difficult than ever, although the labour members of the Second Duma did their best to defend the labour cause there ; Pokrovsky, a labour member, in his speech in the Duma, warned the Government that all attempts to stop the natural growth of labour organisations would only complicate the political atmosphere of the country, and that the development of industrial life in Russia was impossible without the corresponding development of labour organisations. But these protests did not produce any positive results.†

Trade union membership and the payment of fees were rapidly declining. In 1907 there were in Moscow 46 unions with 48,000 members : in 1909 this number decreased to 21 unions with 7,000 members. In St. Petersburg, instead of 44 unions with 51,782 members

* STRENGTH OF TRADE UNIONS

Size of Unions		No. of Unions	Membership
More than 5,000 members	. . .	6	54,293
From 4,000–5,000 „	. . . .	4	17,718
„ 3,000–4,000 „	. . . .	5	17,909
„ 2,000–3,000 „	. . . .	7	8,574
„ 1,000–2,000 „	. . . .	23	33,822
„ 700–1,000 „	. . . .	21	19,212
„ 500– 700 „	. . . .	24	15,349
„ 400– 500 „	. . . .	33	14,845
„ 300– 400 „	. . . .	30	10,740
„ 200– 300 „	. . . .	42	9,658
„ 100– 200 „	. . . .	108	15,430
Less than 100 „	. . . .	349	15,000

(D. Koltsov. " In the Liberation Movement," Vol. I., p. 278.)

† " The Voice of the Social Democrat." Geneva, 1909, No. 18, p. 7.

in 1907, on July 1st, 1908, there were left only 28 unions with 29,300 members.*

The strike movement also slackened. In 1907 740,000 workers took part in strikes, or 41·9 per cent. of all industrial workers; in 1908 only 176,000 workers were involved in strikes, or 9·7 per cent.; in 1909, 64,000, or 3·5 per cent.; and in 1910, 46,000, or 2·4 per cent. The character of strikes changed also. In 1907, 60 per cent. of all strikes were strikes of aggression, for better pay and better working conditions; in 1909 the percentage in this category fell to 15·9. " Defensive " strikes, on the other hand, rose from 14·2 per cent. in 1907 to 38·7 per cent. in 1909. The results of strikes were also much less satisfactory in comparison with 1907: only 48·5 per cent. of strikes ended in favour of the workers in 1909, whereas for 1906 this percentage stood as high as 66·3.

The labour press described the position of trade unions at that time as follows: " Our Union," wrote *The Textile Weaving Loom* in 1909, " is far from being a permanent organisation. The membership of the union resembles rather a crowd of wandering gypsies than a properly organised body. . . . For every ten members who pay their dues regularly, there are 25 temporary members who pay dues only during the first few months." " Our Society," wrote *Printing Affairs* " does not live at all, it simply exists. . . . There is not a penny left for the satisfaction of the cultural needs of our members, for help to the unemployed or for any kind of activities in connection with the defence of workers' rights."†

Some of the trade unions tried to develop mutual

---

* M. Balabanov, " From 1905 to 1917." Moscow, *Gosizdat*, 1927, p. 107, etc.
† M. Balabanov, *op. cit.*, p. 108.

assistance and to carry on the functions of a friendly society. But "in the present state of affairs the work of mutual assistance cannot save the trade unions," wrote the *Goldsmiths' Union*. "Our society has developed these functions, but it still has no funds and membership of the union has not increased. . . . The cause of weakness lies not in the exercise of certain functions by the trade unions, but in the general labour conditions in Russia."*

It would not be far from the truth to say that the trade union movement ceased to exist in Russia at the end of 1909 and the beginning of 1910.

* *Ibid.*, p. 109.

CHAPTER IX

ON THE EVE OF THE WORLD WAR

The Recovery of Russian Industry from the Depression—The Miners' Strike in the Lena Goldfields and their Claims—Delegates and *Starostas*—The Insurance Act of 1912—The Aspirations of Workmen before the War.

AT the end of 1910 Russia began to recover from the depression ; the building industry was the first to recover, then followed the textile and metal industries. The strike movement also awoke to activity. In 1910 already 75,000 workers were involved in strikes, but the majority of these were carried on without any help of the trade unions. The strikes bore a purely economic character, and did not have any political significance up to the moment when the delegates began to be arrested. The arrests of strikers' representatives converted these purely " economic " strikes into so-called " political " strikes for the release of the imprisoned delegates ; to these demands other claims of a general character were added, such as for instance freedom of organisation, an eight-hour working day, etc.

In addition to this, several strikes were called as a protest against capital punishment ; these were inspired by Tolstoy's famous pamphlet, " I cannot keep silent any longer ! " In St. Petersburg the signatures of 2,500 workers were collected for the petition to the Duma protesting against capital punishment, and in Moscow 18,000 workers called a two-day strike on the same issue. The civil funeral of Tolstoy, at his estate " Yassnaya Polyana," at which many thousands of students, workmen, trade unionists and peasants were present, struck the present writer by its highly idealistic spirit, its order, and the devotion shown to the great philosopher. The aspirations of the youth of that time were as high as the political aspirations of the modern *Komsomol* (" The Union of the Communist Youth ") movement in the U.S.S.R. with this difference only, that the latter have vast possibilities and Government encouragement for the attainment of their aspirations, whereas the former were obliged to conceal their real aims until better days should come.

All this gave great stimulus to the reappearance of trade unions and to the steady growth of the strike movement, and there was hope that the Russian trade unions would be able to enlarge their activities, acquire greater influence over the workers and take a more active part in the conflicts between capital and labour. And this would certainly have been the case had Russian social and economic life not been disturbed by events in the Siberian gold-mining area and by the attitude of the Government towards them.

The dispute in question took place in 1912 and reminded everybody of the events of January 9th, 1905, when Gapon led the unarmed workers to the Tsar's Palace. Here again the unarmed crowd of strikers, protesting against bad food and onerous conditions of work, was massacred without warning. According to the Report of Senator Manukhin, 170 workers were killed and 372 injured when a crowd of 6,000 strikers were on their way to the Nadezhdinsky coal-mines to see the Public Prosecutor and ask him to liberate some arrested delegates. When the first shot was fired, says Manukhin's Report, many workers were sitting on a fence or standing by the roadside smoking cigarettes. Eleven of those on the fence, and fourteen others were killed.*

The main causes of the conflict were, according to the same Report of Senator Manukhin, as follows :

1. The Lena Goldfields Company used all means—legal and illegal—to get the highest possible profits.
2. The Company did not introduce the necessary improvements in the mines, and constantly postponed their introduction.
3. Wages were often arbitrarily reduced by the administration.
4. The stores which supplied workers with provisions were yielding a 12 per cent. profit to the Company.
5. The treatment of miners was bad and inhuman.
6. The contracts concluded with workers were greatly to the disadvantage of the latter.
7. The strike had a purely economic background.†

From the very beginning of the strike the miners created a general miners' organisation headed by delegates and *starostas*. The latter were elected on the following basis :

1. The inhabitants of each barrack elect a *starosta* by direct (*i.e.*, by raising hands) or secret ballot.
2. Each *starosta* has two properly elected assistants.
3. The *starosta* is the head of the barrack and can be recalled only on the decision of the Soviet of Starostas.
4. *Starostas* are responsible for any disorders, drunkenness in barracks, etc.
5. All inhabitants of barracks must obey the *starostas'* orders.
6. The Soviet of Starostas is responsible to the delegates.‡

The delegates represented different mines and works and formed the Central Bureau, which enjoyed the full confidence of the miners and which presented

* The Lena Goldfields Company (Lensoto) was formed in 1896 and after 1908 was financed from London by the Lena Goldfields Ltd. M. Balabanov, " From 1905 to 1917," p. 166.
† The *Red Chronicle*, 1930, No. 2 (35), p. 47.
‡ The *Proletarian Revolution*, 1927, No. 4 (63), p. 144.

to the administration of mines the following declaration :

" On 3 March 1912 a General Meeting of workers engaged in the Lena Goldfields decided to cease work until their claims are satisfied. During the strike all workers must get full pay and nobody must be victimised, as the strike is the result of the workers' extreme need and of the refusal by the administration to satisfy their claims. . . . We wish the strike to proceed peacefully, and we hereby give warning that we shall call a general strike of miners in the event of any reprisals being taken against our delegates."*

* The declaration insisted also on the following guarantees for the delegates :

1. The supply of free railway tickets to the delegates for the whole period of negotiations with the Administration.

2. The guarantee of their freedom from arrests.

3. The right to use the People's House for meetings.

4. The employment of new men only with the consent of the delegates.

The claims of miners were as follows :

" 1. During strikes food must be provided in the factory eating-rooms as usual.

" 2. Provisions must be supplied to all workers on the same basis and on the same conditions as to the administration of the mines.

" The distribution of food must take place in the presence of workers' representatives. Meat must be sorted.

" ' Kvass ' (home-made Russian cider) must be provided during the summer months free of charge. Black bread must be of the first quality. Potatoes and cabbages must be served every day, especially because the latter are very good as a cure for scurvy.

" 3. The barracks must be reconstructed at the employers' expense so that there will be enough air and light. Bachelors should be two in a room, and married people should have one room per family. There must be a separate laundry and separate premises for drying washing.

" 4 (a) Skilled workers must not be employed on work other than that for which they are qualified. Miners must not be employed permanently in the same mines.

" (b) All contracts with workmen must be terminated in the summer only. In case of the discharge of a workman, he and his family must be supplied with free railway ticket as far as the Zhigalov Station.

" 5. An 8-hour working day and 7 hours on the eve of Saints'

The administration of the mines did not pay any attention to this warning, some of the delegates were arrested, and the unauthorised order of Captain Treshchenkov to open fire on the crowd without proper warning produced great indignation all over Russia and Siberia.

Again and again we find here the same characteristic features of the strike which we have traced all through the history of the Russian Labour Movement. The strike at first proceeded peacefully, being purely economic in character ; then the police intervened and it immediately assumed a political aspect, and was treated as a riot and a mutiny. The conduct

Days. Work on Sundays must not be compulsory. Work on Sundays and festivals must only be carried on between 6 a.m. and 1 p.m., and at the following rates of pay : the first two hours must be counted as three hours of an ordinary working day, and each successive hour as two hours.

" 6. Increase of wages by 10 to 30 per cent.

" 7. Every miner must have a card indicating the amount of work done during the day. Monthly reports on work done, duly checked, must be posted up in the workshops.

" 8. Monthly payment of wages. Introduction of receipts for the wage paid.

" 9. The foremen must get their supplies three days before the miners.

" 10. Abolition of fines.

" 11. Separate administration for mechanical workers.

" 12. No reduction in rates of time-wages. Work commissioned at distant mines must be paid at rate and a half.

" 13. All workers must get medical assistance as soon as applied for. Full wages must be paid during illness caused through the fault of the administration. In all other cases of illness half wages must be paid. Every patient must have the right to receive a medical certificate of ill-health.

" 14. The discharge of workers must take place only after consultation with the workers' commission.

" 15. Women may be employed only of their own free will.

" 16. The administration must be polite and must address everybody : ' you,' instead of : ' thou.'

" 17. The following persons in the administration are to be discharged (26 names were indicated in the petition).

" 18. Nobody is to be victimised for the strike."

(See V. Vladimirov, " The Events in Lena." Moscow, 1932, pp. 30–32.)

of the strike was from the very beginning in the hands of a self-appointed workers' organisation. We find here the same institution of *starostas*, enjoying the same authority as the *starostas* of the *artels* in peaceful times ; the same delegates, elected by the workmen ; the same belief in the righteousness of their protest and claims, and the same insistence on truth and justice only. The revolutionary parties and the political exiles in Siberia, according to the Report of Senator Manukhin, had not taken a direct part in the movement ; and the miners themselves, in their petition to the Chief Mining Engineer, Tulchinsky, declared that " there are no propagandists or instigators among us, and the police have no right to suspect our legally elected delegates of revolutionary propaganda."*

The strike of the Siberian miners took place, as we have already mentioned, at a moment when Russian industry was recovering from a depression, when the labour movement was becoming more active and society was beginning to pay more attention to the social and political life of the country. The response, therefore, to events in the Lena Goldfields was very great everywhere. There were outbreaks of strikes, and much insistence upon the punishment of those responsible for the massacre, and demands for guarantees that such acts would not occur again.†

The Government fully realised the danger of the increase of revolutionary aspirations, and tried to divert the attention of workmen from political problems by promising to improve the material con-

* V. Vladimirov, " The Events in Lena." Moscow, *Gosizdat*, 1932, p. 32.
† There were, according to employers' statistics, more than 200,000 workers involved in strikes at that time ; the figures of the factory inspectors were 232,000, and the labour press gave as many as 500,000. (M. Balabanov, *op. cit.*, p. 173.)

ditions of the workers' life. " Labour legislation with us," said A. A. Makarov, the Minister of the Interior, in a confidential circular, " is quite a new phenomenon without historical precedent, and the working classes are very much under the influence of revolutionary parties who exploit them in their own interest. But the working classes have realised from former experience that the main burden of strikes is carried on their own shoulders and have ceased to believe in revolutionary slogans. The present moment is therefore very opportune for withholding the working masses from revolutionary activity by introducing Insurance legislation. . . . But on the other hand, the Insurance Act will put large sums of money at the disposal of the insured . . . and it is therefore very important that at the outset practical work should be so organised that the influence of revolutionary parties will be paralysed."*

The Government, guided by these considerations, promulgated in 1912 a new Insurance Act for sick and disabled workers. This Act was no doubt a step forward compared with the Act of 1903, but it was still very unsatisfactory and bore every sign of having been the work of hidebound officials. Its chief drawback was that it applied only to a narrow circle of workers. All employed in home industries, in enterprises with less than twenty people, all agricultural labourers, workers in the building industry as well as workers in Siberia and Turkestan, were excluded from the right to be insured. The administration of the Act was placed entirely in the hands of the employers, without any participation of workers in

* M. Korfut, " The 1912 Insurance Act," in the *Red Chronicle*, 1928, No. 1 (25), p. 163. " The better the workers are safeguarded financially," wrote S. P. Beletsky, the Vice-President of the Department of the Police, " the less will the mass of the working population be influenced by revolutionary propaganda." (*Ibid.*, p. 139.)

it. They were not allowed direct representation in the insurance offices, but were offered, instead, the privilege of nominating candidates only.

The Insurance Act of 1912 met with great opposition from the workers, but the majority of them did not boycott the Act at first ; on the contrary, they urged that the Government scheme should be taken up and used as one of the means of developing labour organisation.*

Soon after the promulgation of the Insurance Act, some of the workers' delegates, who criticised the Act, were arrested and this naturally irritated the workers, who then began to boycott the insurance offices. The Government realised that the Insurance Act, instead of calming the working masses, only served to anger them the more. Maklakov, the Minister of the Interior, together with S. J. Timashev, the Minister of Trade, decided therefore to suspend the formation of the insurance offices until the autumn of 1913. Meantime, the grave economic situation caused the strike movement to develop at the end of 1913 and the beginning of 1914 to such an

---

* According to the Report of the St. Petersburg Police Department of December 19th, 1912, " the measures taken by the Government to put the Insurance Act into operation are meeting with growing opposition from the workers of the Petersburg factories who are supported by the central organisation of the Social Democratic Party.

" The leading groups of *Mensheviks*, according to information received, passed a resolution in which they recommended :

" 1. The recall of those workers' representatives whom the Government had appointed to the Insurance Council.

" 2. The convening of an All-Russian Congress of workers for electing representatives to the Insurance Council.

" 3. The calling of a conference of worker-electors of the Labour Members of the Duma and the election by them of temporary representatives to the Insurance Council."

The Report also described the attitude of *Mensheviks* and *Leninists* toward the Insurance Act. The *Red Chronicle*, 1928, No. 1 (25), pp. 157–158 ; The *Proletarian Revolution*, 1928, No. 2 (73) p. 90.

extent that the Government, being engaged with the strike movement, was not anxious to put the law into practice.*

The growth of strike movement, especially in the first half of 1914, greatly alarmed the employers. This, however, was a source of rejoicing to the left wing of the Social-Democratic Party : in the increase of " political " strikes they saw the advent of a new era, the awakening of the Russian proletariat, and its readiness to follow entirely the path of political struggle. The political side of the labour movement seemed now to the industrial workmen to be also of great importance. The combined efforts of the Siberian miners, the success of their general organisation, headed by delegates and *starostas* and a collective protest all over Russia against the Insurance Act, drew the attention of workmen once more to the idea of a general workers' organisation similar to the Soviet of Workers' Deputies in 1905, which represented the whole body of workers. This idea became popular again, and was universal among Russian workmen in the first half of 1914, and especially just before the declaration of the War.

* The celebration of May 1st, which was always very popular in Russia, as a national spring festival, caused also a good deal of trouble to the police. It is interesting to note here that the employers were not in favour of fining or discharging workmen for striking on that day, as they were afraid to lose the labour force, which was so needed during the improving conditions in industry.

CHAPTER X

DURING THE WAR

The Declaration of the War and its Effects on the Labour Supply—
The Strike Movement during the War—" Political " Strikes—Trade
Unions—The Shadow of Zubatov—Declarations of the Fourth Duma.

THE Russian industry was just recovering from the
depression when the War was declared ; the demand
for labour was steadily increasing, which in turn
invigorated the Labour Movement. But all this was
naturally changed beyond recognition immediately
after the entry of Russia into the War. The mining
industry, for instance, in the Donets Basin, suffered
a great exodus of workers. An exodus of workers
also took place in the Urals, where the mines lost,
after the first mobilisation, up to 12·3 per cent. of
the total number of workers. The textile industry
experienced similar trouble.

According to the Factory Inspectors' Reports,
" Immediately after the outbreak of hostilities, an
unreasonable panic seized manufacturers. Enormous
reductions in output took place simultaneously in all
industries. Large, as well as small, factories tried to
fix a minimum output by reducing the working time,
shortening the number of hours worked per day or
the number of days per week. In consequence, the
output in all groups of industry decreased by 25 and
even 50 per cent."*

The effect of the declaration of the War on the

* S. P. Turin, " Wages in Russia during the War." Moscow,
1915 ; In the " Materials as to the Rise of Prices during the War,"
published by the University of Moscow. Vol. III., p. 217.

strike movement was also very great. It suddenly created among the workers a kind of collective impulse to stop the movement in view of an approaching calamity. And the strike movement ceased immediately. The collective will of the working population accomplished what no compulsory measures of any kind would have been able to bring about.

But this did not last long. The strike movement revived again in 1915 and 1916. But this time it was mainly a struggle for better wages, shorter hours, better conditions of work and a better standard of life. Strikes on political grounds also increased, but at the beginning they were of much shorter duration. In order to avoid any misrepresentation of the labour movement in Russia during the War, we mention below some of the typical strikes in 1915 and 1916. All of them in the war-time atmosphere were considered by the Government to be of a dangerous " political " character.*

*   STRIKES IN 1915

1. In January, several strikes occurred in Petrograd and Riga in commemoration of January 9th, 1905.
2. The expulsion of the Labour Members of the Duma caused several strikes in Moscow. There was also a strike in Moscow in celebration of the abolition of serfdom on February 19th, 1861.
3. In Kharkov there was a strike against the introduction of the Insurance Act, owing to the false rumour that the deductions from wages for the sick fund would be made retrospective over the last ten years.
4. The fall of the fortress of Przemysl caused several patriotic strikes in Petrograd and Reval.
5. In Saratov on the same occasion the railwaymen arranged a demonstration, carrying the portrait of the Tsar, and the whole population of the town joined in.[1]
6. May Day was celebrated by a one-day strike in Petrograd, Rostov on Don, Samara, Saratov, Tver and Kharkov.
7. In August all the cotton mills of Ivanovo-Voznesensk were affected by strikes, which split the working population into two

---

[1] V. Antonov-Saratovsky, " The Proletarian Struggle." Moscow, *Gosizdat*, 1925, p. 11.

The trade union movement practically ceased to exist during the War. Sixty-nine trade unions, according to the journal, *The Freedom of Unions*, were shut down by the Administration just before and at the beginning of the War, and during 1915 forty-nine applications for the registration of new unions were turned down.*

There were at the same time some attempts, similar to that of Zubatov and Ushakov, to influence the labour movement in Russia. On December 2nd, 1915, the first number of the *Russian Worker* appeared. The editors of this weekly periodical were P. A. Moscaluk, a member of the Duma, and a journalist, V. Zaborovsky, both Conservatives. The acting-editor of the journal was Mme. Elisabeth Bork-

groups : the minority (the more advanced workers), looked upon the strike as a protest against the War, the majority were against the strike. This led to several conflicts between the two groups ; the police interfered, and with the help of a military force, dispersed the crowd, wounding and killing several workers.

8. Several strikes occurred in September and October in Petrograd, Moscow and many other places as a protest against the intention of the Government to dissolve the Duma and against the decision of the Government to call up the Second Army Reserve.

9. The employment of prisoners of war in factories, the practice of sending strikers to the Front, the prohibition of meetings in connection with the participation of workers in the work of War Industrial Committees : all these causes brought about strikes in many places during November and December 1915.

STRIKES IN 1916

The strikes were called either in commemoration of January 9th, 1905, or as a protest against arrests of labour representatives and the prohibition of meetings. There were many strikes also of German and Austrian prisoners of War, who objected to being employed in making munitions. In October 1916 a rather large number of strikes was recorded : 119, in which 138,531 men were involved ; the majority of them (115) occurred in Petrograd. The chief cause of these strikes was the shortage of food.[1]

---

[1] " The Labour Movement during the War." Moscow, Centrarkhiv, 1926, p. 19, etc.

* M. Balabanov, *op. cit.*, p. 336 (footnote). See also: A. Elnitsky, " History of the Labour Movement." Moscow, 1925, p. 201.

Shabelsky, who was also the editor of a Monarchist paper, *Freedom and Order*. This paper carried on a vigorous campaign against social-democratic ideas : " Our Russian social-democrats," wrote the *Russian Worker* in its issue No. 22, " are hired agents of Germany. . . . They are stirring up strife and sedition. . . . Our Government cannot cope with them and we, non-party workers, ought to get rid of . . . these political charlatans."*

Meantime the discontent in the country was spreading, and thirty-one members of the Fourth Duma made the following declaration on June 14th, 1916 :

" The strike movement among the working population is growing every day. In Petrograd nearly all the big undertakings were affected by strikes during the first half of 1916. . . . In the provinces the movement is becoming more and more intense. . . . In the majority of cases the workers insist on higher wages. . . . The disparity between low wages and high prices is evident. . . . The main feature of strikes is their mass character. All professions and groups of the working population are affected by the movement. Even the punishment of strikers by hard labour does not stop it.

" This movement, which is a sign of the great discontent of the working population with their conditions of work and life, takes the form of an unorganised mass protest owing to the absence of the trade unions.

" The usual course of strikes is as follows : The factory administration declares a lockout after the strike has broken out. The military authorities then intervene and send the strikers either into the Army or into the disciplinary battalions. . . . At Niko-

* The *Red Chronicle*. *Gosizdat*, 1930, No. 2 (35), p. 110.

layev, for instance, 7,500 strikers out of the 14,000 employees at the ' Naval ' works were sent to the Front. Then, after the strike was over, it was discovered that the works could not carry on owing to the absence of skilled labour. The same thing happened in the Putilov works.

" Workers are not allowed to hold meetings . . . and the activities of trade unions are limited to a minimum. . . . The Police Department, in its recent Report, holds the labour delegates on the War Industrial Committees responsible for the organisation of the strike movement. . . . At the same time the employers largely utilise the system of ' black lists.' The Association of Employers in Petrograd, for instance, issued the following circular letter, dated 22 March 1916, No. 181 :

' Dear Sirs, The Council of the Association cordially invites its members, owing to the strike at the works of G. A. Lessner & Co. Ltd., to abstain from giving employment in their factories to workers formerly employed by the above company.'

" The same thing happened in Moscow, where a similar circular was issued by the Moscow Employers Association, which united 818 factories employing 381,000 men. The members of this Association were asked not to employ 67 persons formerly employed by the General Electric Company."*

On December 8th, 1916, thirty members of the Duma returned again to the question of trade unions in Russia. Their declaration read as follows :

" The Allied Governments, as well as our enemies, fully realise the importance of the workers' aspirations and are trying to create favourable conditions for the development of the productive forces of their

* " The Labour Movement during the War." Moscow, 1926, pp. 295, etc.

countries, whereas our Government is engaged in disorganising our working masses. The labour press is abolished, the trade unions are closed, the health insurance offices are paralysed in their activities. . . . The desire of workers to take an active part in the work of War Industrial Committees is meeting with constant resistance on the part of the Central Administration. . . . Arrests of labour delegates to these Committees take place nearly everywhere. In Samara, for instance, the whole labour delegation to the War Industrial Committee was exiled to Siberia and Turkestan. Half of the newly elected delegates in Saratov were arrested on the very day of their election.

" Nearly all the trade unions were closed down at the beginning of the War and the winding-up of those remaining is proceeding apace . . . "*

A few months later, on February 14th, 1917, almost on the eve of the February Revolution, the Social-Democratic Members of the Duma again raised the question of the Government's attitude towards the labour organisations, pointing out that all the trade unions had been shut down by the Administration, " that the consumers' co-operative societies are closely watched by the police and the health insurance offices are under the constant supervision of civil and military authorities."†

The only organisations, which became centres for the working population at that time, were the War Industrial Committees. Participation in these was advocated by all who were engaged in practical work among the labouring classes. The left wing and even some of the right wing of the Social Demo-

---

* *Ibid.*, p. 310. Amongst those who signed the declaration, we find the following names, which are known in this country : Kerensky, Chkheidze, Shingarev and Milyukov.
† M. Balabanov, *op. cit.*, p. 336.

crats looked upon the participation of workers in the War Industrial Committees with suspicion. They did not see that the committees were, after all, a very good school for the workmen and made them more capable to face the responsibilities imposed upon them by the outbreak of the Revolution.*

When the Revolution broke out and the machinery of Government collapsed entirely, the Russian workers in revolt realised that they did not have any political or economic organisations of their own round which they could unite. And no wonder that the appeal for the creation of a " Soviet of Soldiers', Sailors', Workers' and Peasants' Deputies " found a ready response in the exhausted Russian Army, hurrying away from the Front, in the war-weary urban population and in the vast masses of illiterate peasantry, all of whom were suffering from the shortage of food and from the complete disorganisation of the economic life of the country.

The outbreak of the Revolution did not come as a surprise to us, Russians. Peter Kropotkin was right when he said in his " Open Letter to the Western Working Men," written on the day of his departure to Russia, that :

" If the Russian nation has succeeded in driving away her autocrats, with their bureaucratic sequel, and if it has managed to conquer in a few days this first basis of all social reconstruction—political equality of all citizens—it was the reconstruction work which was going on all over Russia since the beginning of the War, which has helped to do so. It was due to voluntary effort and free initiative, and

---

* The present writer talked of the importance of these at the beginning of 1916 with some Russian Social Democrats in Norway and Sweden, and to the " political *émigrés* " in London, but all of them were for the boycott of the War Industrial Committees.

it was *this* work which rendered the revolution possible and actually unavoidable."*

---

* Typewritten copy left with S. P. Turin. P. Kropotkin went to Russia on June 4th, 1917, under my name, in order to avoid capture by a German submarine, said to have been watching for him, and he disclosed his own name only after crossing the North Sea.

EPILOGUE

THE Revolution of February 1917 stirred great hopes in the Russian labour organisations. Trade unions reappeared like mushrooms. At the same time, and often independently of the trade unions, factory committees (soviets of *starostas* or delegates) were rapidly set up in all factories and workshops. The first factory committees, according to their rules, were organs for the defence of the economic, professional and cultural interests of workers. " The Factory Committees," it was said in the Rules of the Moscow Factory Committees " must also, in view of the weakness of the trade unions, undertake the organisation of strikes and leadership in the economic struggle of the workers."

The Petersburg Soviet of Workers' Deputies, in its Agreement with the Society of Factory Owners, made during the second week after the outbreak of the Revolution, defined the duties of factory committees as follows :

The representation of workers' interests in Government and public institutions, the working out of schemes as to the improvement of the social economic life of workers, the settlement of disputes amongst the workmen themselves and the representation of workers' interests in the disputes with the employers. The factory committees, according to the Agreement, must be elected in every factory and workshop on the basis of universal, equal, direct and secret ballot. Later on, in May 1917, the First Conference of the Factory Committees accepted " Workers Control " as the main function of factory committees,* and on the 14th November, 1917, Lenin and the People's Commissar for Labour (Shlyapnikov) signed a decree, according to which

" The Workers' Control organs have the right to supervise production, establish the minimum output of the undertaking and take measures to ascertain the cost of production of articles.

" The Workers' Control organs have the right to control all the business correspondence of the undertaking ; owners of undertakings concealing correspondence are liable to prosecution. Commercial secrets are abolished. Owners are obliged to submit their books and accounts for the current year as well as for previous years to the control committees. The decisions of the Workers' Control organs are binding upon the owners, and can only be altered by an order of the higher Workers' Control organs."†

At the beginning of the Revolution the factory committees were obliged to deal at once with the problem of factory management, as the majority of employers, with their technical staffs and even foremen, left the factories during the revolutionary days of March 1917. The factory committees began to issue orders as to production, disposal of raw

---

* " The Labour Movement in 1917." Moscow, *Gosizdat*, 1926, pp. 40, 75, 320. See also pp. 342–351 for the Rules of the Factory Committees, prepared by the Central Soviet of the Factory Committees.

† " Trade Unions in Soviet Russia," A collection of Russian Trade Union documents compiled by the I. L. P. Information Committee, London, 1920, p. 20.

materials, fuel, machinery, etc. Each factory committee was concerned with the interests of its own
undertaking only, and often the prices of goods
produced were raised without regard to market
prices. Then the Provisional Government attempted
to restrict their activities, but nobody paid any
attention to this, and in the end the factory committees took the control of industry entirely into
their own hands.

The factory committees after a while actually
" ended by disorganising the whole of the national
economy as, in order to obtain raw materials and
fuel for their own requirements, they sent agents
into the provinces who often bought at ridiculously
high prices."* The situation soon became very
alarming, as the factory committees " began to
claim that they owned the factories, thus converting
the workers into a new body of private share-
holders."†

The trade unions had foreseen this danger and
tried to regain control over the factory committees.
At the Third Conference of Trade Unions in June
1917, consisting mainly of the menshevik delegates,
this result had been partly achieved ; but the
minority of the Conference, representing bolshevik
delegates, insisted on the postponement of the taking
over of the control of factory committees by the
trade unions, because they hoped that later on the
Bolshevik Party would have greater influence upon
both. They succeeded in this at the First Trade
Union Congress in January 1918, and it was then
decided to amalgamate the Central Association of

* Ryazanov, " The Verbatim ·Report of the First Trade Union
Congress.' Cited by Zagorsky in " The Trade Union Movement in
Soviet Russia." Geneva, 1927, p. 52.
† " Russia : The Official Report of the British Trades Union
Delegation in November 1924." London, p. 138.

Factory Committees with the central trade union organisation.*

Later, the activities of factory committees in the sphere of industrial management were more restricted and their representation on the management was reduced to one-third (the other two-thirds being held by the trade unions and by the Supreme Economic Council). In 1920 the Third Congress of Trade Unions deprived factory committees of any share at all in factory management. The trade unions themselves were, about this time, converted into State organs, and menshevist opposition was suppressed.

This process of evolution of the Russian labour organisation was preceded by a prolonged struggle of the trade unions of the old type with the policy of the bolsheviks. Some of the documents found by the present writer among the materials of the Labour Information Bureau in London, and which have not been made known in this country, clearly indicate that the right wing of the Russian Social-Democratic Party (mensheviks) did not believe in the possibility of introducing a Socialist order in Russia imme-

---

* The First Trade Union Congress " made the Factory Committees local units of the Trade Union by applying generally and compulsorily the principle of One Factory, One Union. This meant that every worker in one factory, whatever his occupation, joined the union to which the factory belonged. For example, in a machine tool factory, not only were the carpenters and bricklayers employed on factory repairs made to join the Metal Workers' Union, but so also were the cooks. In the same way railway repair shopmen join the Railwaymen's Union and railway stock builders join the Metal Workers' Union. This principle of ' One Factory, One Union,' has become a permanent part of the soviet system. One result of it is the getting rid of all overlapping and competition between unions— another is the division of unionism into 23 national industrial unions which are permanent and not as elsewhere constantly amalgamating and seceding." (" Russia : The Official Report of the British Trades Union Delegation to Russia," p. 138.) There are at present 154 trade unions in the U.S.S.R., which were formed out of forty-seven trade unions existing last year (1934).

diately after the Revolution, and considered the Revolution of 1917 as a bourgeois-democratic revolution only. In the opinion of the majority of trade unionists who gathered at the Third All-Russian Conference of Trade Unions in June 1917, the Russian Revolution was only a bourgeois-democratic revolution, but not a Socialist revolution : " The Revolution must make of Russia, politically and economically, a European country. Our backward labour movement must become a European one also. It must acquire the same forms of organisation as those in the highly developed capitalist countries of Europe. This applies to our political life as well as to the trade union movement."*

The Conference, in accordance with these views, passed a resolution, in which the principles of trade union organisation were laid down on the lines of European practice and of Russian experience. The independence and unity of the trade union movement and its affiliation to the Trade Union Inter-

* The Third All-Russian Conference of Trade Unions met in Petrograd on June 20th, 1917. There were 247 delegates present, representing 976 trade unions, and fifty-one trades councils with a total membership of 1,475,429. The structure of the Conference, according to the trades represented, was as follows :

Metal workers	.	.	.	400,000
Textile workers	.	.	.	178,560
Printers	.	.	.	55,291
Tailors	.	.	.	51,545
Carpenters and Joiners		.		28,601
Clerks	.	.	.	45,981
Other trades		.	.	715,451
Total		.	.	1,475,429

(" The Labour Movement in 1917." Moscow, *Gosizdat*, 1926, p. 85) ; P. Kolokolnikov, " The Trade Union Movement in Russia." Petrograd, 1917, p. 10. The Conference represented about 75 per cent. of all trade unionists in Russia. Many provincial trade unions (like the printers, coal-miners and others), were not represented at the Conference.

national were proclaimed as the fundamental aim of the Russian Labour Movement.*

Within the next six months the relative strength of the two wings of the Social-Democratic Party in the trade union movement underwent a complete change. At the First All-Russian Trade Union Congress in January 1918 the majority of the delegates were already bolsheviks.†

The Congress proclaimed new principles for the Russian Trade Union Movement, condemned the principle of " party neutrality " as being bourgeois, and, instead of the independence of the trade union

* For the full text of the resolution, see " The Labour Movement in 1917," p. 89. The Conference passed several useful resolutions (on the industrial principle of organisation, on unemployment, women's labour, factory inspection, conciliation boards and industrial courts, co-operative societies, the eight-hour day, etc.), and established the *All-Russian Central Council of Trade Unions* (A.C.C.T.U. or A.U.C.C.T.U. or (in Russian) V.TS.S.P.S.).

† There were at this First Congress 416 delegates representing 2,532,000 members. Their distribution according to the various trades was as follows :

Metal workers	.	.	.	600,000
Textile workers	.	.	.	500,000
Printers	.	.	.	90,000
Clerks	.	.	.	180,000
Leather workers	.	.	.	200,000
Workers in food trades		.		120,000
Other trades	.	.	.	842,000
Total		.	.	2,532,000

The distribution of the delegates according to the various political parties was as follows :

Bolsheviks	.	.	.	.	273
Mensheviks	.	.	.	.	61
Social Revolutionaries		.		.	31
Maximalists and Anarkho-Syndicalists		.			12
Non-Party	.	.	.	.	39
Total	.	.	.	.	416

(" The Verbatim Report of the First All-Russian Trade Union Congress." Moscow, 1918, p. 338.)

movement, declared that the unions ought to become " organs subordinated to the Socialist Power."*

At the Second Trade Union Congress in 1919 Lenin endorsed this view, and defined the functions of trade unions as follows : " To-day it is already insufficient for us to limit ourselves to proclaiming the dictatorship of the proletariat. It is inevitable to give a State character to the trade unions, inevitable to merge them with the organs of State power, inevitable that the building of large-scale industry should pass completely into their hands."†

Two years passed after this Congress. The so-called " War Communism " and Red Terror were in full swing, and it seemed that all the former aspirations and illusions of the trade unionists of the old school had been swept away. But when a delegation from the British Labour Party and Trades Union Congress arrived in Russia as late as May 1920, the Russian Printers' Union called a general meeting in order to welcome the delegation and to express directly to them their hopes, their sorrows and their aspirations.‡

The general meeting of printers took place on May 23rd, 1920, and after greetings to the British Delegation and speeches from J. Skinner, A. Purcell and others, a declaration to the British Labour Delegation was passed by the meeting with two

* " The Verbatim Report of the First Trade Union Congress," p. 5.

† " Lenin on Democracy and the Trade Unions." London, 1934, p. 15.

‡ The members of the delegation who represented the Labour Party were Mrs. Philip Snowden, Messrs. Robert Williams and Ben Turner, while Miss Margaret Bondfield and Messrs. A. A. Purcell and J. H. Skinner represented the Parliamentary Committee of the Trades Union Congress, with Dr. L. Haden Guest as Secretary and Medical Adviser, and Mr. C. Roden Buxton as interpreter.

dissentients and four abstentions. The Communists ostentatiously left the hall.*

" All Russian Socialists are convinced," it was said in the Declaration, " that the triumph of Socialism in Russia is possible only if there is a Socialist Revolution in the West. All endeavours to force socialism upon one backward country alone will give no positive results. They will only lead to endless sufferings of the working population. That is why the Russian working class insists on the independent fight against its class enemies and on the independence of the labour organisations, contrary to the wishes of the present ruling power."†

This belief in the impossibility of a Socialist order in a backward country like Russia was shared by Lenin himself up to 1918. At the opening of the First Congress of the Supreme Economic Council in 1918, Lenin said : " We must not forget that we alone cannot achieve a socialist revolution in one country only, even if it were a less backward country than Russia."‡

This prolonged struggle of the old school of trade unionists lasted throughout the whole period of the New Economic Policy (N.E.P.), when the capitalist elements were still alive and strong in the country, and when the Russian worker was still a wage-earner in State and private enterprises. The First Five-Year Plan in Russia (1928–33) opened a new page in the history of the Russian labour organisations : the soviets of delegates and the trade unions themselves

---

* For the full text of the Declaration, see Appendix VII, p. 193. The membership of the Printers' Union came down in the first half of 1920 to 56,300, but it rose again at the beginning of 1921 to 93,900. (" L'Economie de l'Union des R.S.S." Moscow, 1925, p. 514.)
† See Appendix VII, p. 193.
‡ " The Supreme Economic Council." Moscow, 1918, The Verbatim Report, p. 5. (Trudy 1 Vserossiyskago S'ezda Sovietov Narodnago Khozyaistva.)

ceased to be " organs of revolt," and were entrusted with new functions.*

In the foregoing narrative some attempt has been made to describe the main trend of the Labour Movement in Russia with special reference to trade unionism, to trace the causes which brought the Russian labour organisations into existence and to analyse the origins and nature of soviets of delegates which became the prototype of the present soviet system in the U.S.S.R.

The study of relevant sources and personal observation have led us to the following conclusions :

The Russian Labour Movement, as we have already mentioned in the Preface to this book, differed greatly from that of the chief European countries from its inception up to its final stage. On the formal side there are similarities ; the same institutions and organisations bearing the same names, but their substance, their relative weight, their bearing on the whole movement were different. And they were different because the subject of the movement—the Russian worker—and his surroundings were different.

The Russian worker, as we have seen, was first of all a peasant. He did not lose his ties with the country-side during the flourishing period of capitalism in Russia, on the eve of the Revolution of 1905 ; and even five years after the Revolution of 1917—in

---

* Much has been written (in Russian) on trade union problems after the Revolution. They have been discussed in the works of Bukharin, Lenin, Ryazanov, Tomsky, Trotsky and others. The following pamphlets, as an introduction to the study of those problems and of their discussion, may be mentioned here : L. Trotsky, " Functions and Tasks of Trade Unions." Petersburg, *Gosizdat*, 1920. V. Lenin, " On Trade Unions, the Policy of To-day and on Trotsky's Mistake." Petersburg, *Gosizdat*, 1921 ; " Lenin über das Genossenschaftswesen. Pokrowsk. A.S.S.R. der Wolgadeutschen," 1930 ; " Lenin on Democracy and the Trade Unions." London, 1934.

1922—he " considered his occupation in industry as of secondary importance and tried by all means not to lose his ties with the countryside. The working population are still in their spirit and in their interests peasants, and they consider their work in the factories as only a temporary occupation and quite subordinate to their work on the land."*

In addition to this it must be remembered that the Russian worker did not pass through mediævalism and did not inherit a European culture. " In Russia the proletariat did not arise gradually through the ages, carrying with itself the burden of the past as in England, but in leaps involving sharp changes of environment, ties, relations, and a sharp break with the past. It is just this fact—combined with the concentrated oppressions of Tsarism—that made the Russian worker hospitable to the boldest conclusions of revolutionary thought—just as the backward industries were hospitable to the last word in capitalist organisation."†

Another important feature of the Russian Labour Movement is the character of the Russian labour organisation. We have seen that throughout the whole period of the Russian Monarchy and long before the development of the capitalist system in Russia, the Russian worker created his own organisation—the soviet of delegates, called in early days *starostas*—built on the lines of a village community organisation. This institution, though its functions and influence differed at different periods, and though it was always largely exploited for Government and Party purposes, was the *quintessence* of the whole Russian Labour Movement.

---

* L. M. Pumpyansky. Cited in Chapter IV., p. 55.
† Leon Trotsky, "The History of the Russian Revolution." London, 1934, Vol. I., p. 33.

It originated, as we have seen, in the days when all Russians were serfs ; it survived through the reactionary times of Nicholas I. ; after the Emancipation and up to the beginning of the twentieth century it was actually the basic form of labour organisation ; it grew tremendously in the revolutionary days of 1905, guiding the working population and setting up the First Soviet of Workers', Sailors', Soldiers' and Peasants' Deputies. The memory of the First Soviet and its idea were kept deeply hidden in the hearts of the workers throughout the reactionary period of Nicholas II. And the soviets of delegates reappeared with renewed strength in the first days of the February Revolution in 1917 under the name of factory committees.

It was first of all an organisation wider than a mere craft or even industrial union. It was an organisation representing all the workers in a factory, in an industry, or even in a locality. It would be created in spite of the existence of trade unions. The latter represented its own members only, and could not speak with authority on behalf of the whole group of workers involved in or affected by a dispute. Besides, as we have seen, the trade unions in Russia never attained such strength as would permit them to cope effectively with the vast, spontaneous and unorganised Russian Labour Movement.*

The factory workers when forming a soviet of delegates never considered it to be a purely working-class, proletarian organisation, as they never con-

---

* Khrustalev-Nossar, who was the President of the St. Petersburg Soviet of Workers' Deputies in 1905, defined it as an organisation which had replaced the existing trade unions and which had become a kind of confederation of all workers with the functions of trades councils. See Khrustalev-Nossar, " A History of the Soviet of Workers' Deputies." St. Petersburg, pp. 148–150. Cited by P. Gorin in his " Essays on the History of Soviets of Workers' Deputies." Moscow, " The Communist Academy," 1930, p. 98.

sidered themselves to be purely industrial workmen. The majority, as we have seen, had not lost their ties with the countryside, and most of them owned a house with a plot in which their relatives lived or which was let to somebody else in the village. The factory workers held the view that the duty of the soviet of delegates was not only to defend them against exploitation, but also to be the guardian of their civil rights.

In their attitude towards revolutionary and Socialist parties, the soviets of delegates were nominally " non-party " organisations, but actually they were greatly influenced by the revolutionary parties and by their more advanced members, who, as a rule, always had great sympathy with democratic and Socialist ideas. Afanassiev, Khrustalev-Nossar and Moisseyenko, are three of the typical delegates and worker-leaders : the first was a democrat with Socialist tendencies, the second was a social-democrat, and the third became an ardent bolshevik.*

Without close connection with the social-revolutionary and social-democratic organisations and without their assistance the Russian people would not have been able to win the liberties proclaimed by the first Revolution of 1905, and to achieve in 1917 a complete liberation of the Russian peasantry and of industrial workmen from the ugly forms of primitive capitalistic exploitation and from the yoke of an autocratic Government, imbued with the ideas of German militarism and Eastern oligarchy.

The last, and perhaps not the least, peculiarity of the Russian Labour Movement lies in the fact that Russia escaped the bitter class struggle which is to be found in Europe ; but she developed another kind

* See Chapters III., V. and VI.

of struggle of a more general type : the persistent struggle of Government against people.

For two centuries the Russian people were divided into two groups : the rulers and the ruled, " we " and " they." The constant repressions of the ruled by the rulers brought about revolts and rebellions, the outcome of which was the collapse of the Russian Empire. The Revolution of 1917 brought the exploited and oppressed—the ruled—to power and showed them the prospect of a new and fuller life. Events after the Revolution developed with great rapidity. The Provisional Government did not last long ; the Democratic Conference in Moscow did not achieve much and succeeded only, at the suggestion of Prince Peter Kropotkin, in proclaiming the Russian Federative Republic. The Constituent Assembly was dispersed by Lenin and the cry " All Power to the Soviets " was replaced by the Party slogan : " Dictatorship of the Proletariat." This brought about the Civil War, the reign of terror, and so-called " War Communism."*

The problem of " we " and " they " did not disappear during the period of War Communism (1918–21) and during the New Economic Policy (1921–26) ; it only took on a different form. Does it still exist ? There are at present two ruling bodies in the U.S.S.R. ; the All-Union Communist Party of Bolsheviks with its three million members,

---

* Lettres de P. A. Kropotkin à S. P. Turin, 1917–20. " Le Monde Slave." Paris, January, 1925, p. 140 : " Je l'avais proposée sous une forme extrêmement modérée (c'est que jusque là, personne n'avait prononcé le mot ' République '), et notamment en évitant d'empiéter par avance sur les droits de l'Assemblée constituante suprême, simplement pour lui faciliter sa tâche : je demandais à la Conférence d'exprimer son vœu en faveur de la République. Toute la salle fut debout et improvisa une ovation tumultueuse." See also Leon Trotsky, " The History of the Russian Revolution." London, 1934, Vol. II., p. 187.

and the All-Union Congress of Soviets, representing, through the city and village soviets, a
population of over 170 millions. These two bodies
are not identical, and they cannot dissolve each
other. The Congress of Soviets, as a State Power, is
greatly influenced and overshadowed by the Communist Party. Have they solved the problem of
" we " and " they "—the problem upon the right
solution of which depends the future of the Russian
people ?

WORKERS' FAMILY BUDGET ENQUIRIES IN
SOVIET RUSSIA

———

THE CO-OPERATIVE MOVEMENT
IN RUSSIA

WORKERS' FAMILY BUDGET ENQUIRIES IN SOVIET RUSSIA *

THE number of enquiries into workers' family budgets in Russia before the Revolution of 1917 was very small ; such enquiries were conducted chiefly by trade unions, usually in most unfavourable conditions, and therefore presented very limited scope for a thorough investigation of the conditions of the working classes ; moreover, they were confined to certain industries and towns. Such were, for instance, the budget enquiries made in St. Petersburg in 1908 and 1909, in Baku in 1910, and several others. These enquiries—supplemented by official statistics—are the only available sources for the study of the standard of living of Russian workers before the Revolution.

Since the Revolution, workers' family budget enquiries have been conducted in Russia every year. November is chosen as the most convenient and most characteristic month for such investigations. Unfortunately, the budget enquiries of the first years of the Revolution (1918–22) are hardly comparable with each other and with later enquiries, for they were conducted during the civil war and the experiments of pure Communism, when wages had ceased to play any important part in the income of the workers.

* This report of the present writer was published in the *International Labour Review*. Geneva, Vol. XX., No. 4, October 1929. The author takes this opportunity of expressing his thanks to the Editor of the *Review* for permission to reprint this article.
For wages and the prices of food during the years 1901–1915 see Appendix VIII, p. 196.

Before the Revolution wages were the principal source of a worker's income and represented from 93 to 100 per cent. of the total ; during the civil war and so-called " War Communism " (1918–21) wages represented only from 20 to 38 per cent. of the whole income of a married worker, rising to 45·8 per cent. for the unmarried, whose number, by the way, is very small (there are only 5 per cent. of single persons among the workers in the provinces and from 12 to 16 per cent. in the capitals). The New Economic Policy, introduced in 1921, began to show its effects in the following year, and since 1922 wages have been regaining their former position as the chief source of income, of which they now represent 80 to 90 per cent.

The gold rouble was introduced in Russia in 1924, while all previous budget enquiries are made in so-called " Moscow " roubles, based on the " basket " of necessaries used by the Central Bureau of Labour Statistics as a unit for calculating budget indices. This fact causes great difficulties in the comparison of nominal and real wages for the years 1922–24 with wages for later years, when budget enquiries were made in gold roubles (*chervonets*).

Scope of Enquiries

At present, workers' family budget enquiries in Russia are conducted on a large scale, by means of a very detailed questionnaire and with the help of agents, who distribute account books to workers' families and supervise the keeping of records. The Central Statistical Department is assisted by the local offices for labour statistics and also by local trade union committees. Budget enquiries cover four main industrial regions : Moscow, Leningrad, the Ural district, and the Donbas coal-mining area

in the Ukraine, and are collected among workers
employed in the following main groups of industry :
textiles, metals, and coal mining.

The number of returns examined for the last six
years and the average size of the families covered by
them are shown in the following table.

NUMBER OF RETURNS EXAMINED AND AVERAGE SIZE OF FAMILIES, 1922–27 *

Date of enquiry	Number of returns	Average number of persons in a family
December, 1922 . . .	1,434	—
November, 1923 . . .	1,600	4·15
November–December, 1924 .	1,600	3·60–4·21
November, 1925 . . .	1,402	4·10
November, 1926 . . .	1,380	4·10
November, 1927 . . .	1,400	3·93

The small number of returns examined, and the
fact that the returns were made only in certain
districts and certain branches of industry, make it
impossible to consider these budgets as a representative sample of workers' family budgets in Russia ;
they merely represent the regions where they were
collected, and therefore indicate the conditions prevailing in these regions only.

NOMINAL MONTHLY WAGES

It is to be noted in the first place that the wages
given in the enquiry represent the wages of the
aristocracy of labour in the districts in question.

* *Statisticheskoe Obozrénie* (*Statistical Review*), 1927, No. 5, and
1928, No. 5 ; " Narodnoe Khozyaistvo S.S.S.R." (" National
Economy of U.S.S.R."), 1924, p. 546 ; " *Trud v* S.S.S.R." (" Labour
in U.S.S.R."). Moscow, 1926, p. 172.

The figures given by the current statistics for average monthly wages in the same districts are much lower, and those for average monthly wages for the whole of Russia are lower still, as shown by the following figures (chervonets roubles) :

	1925	1926	1927
Budget enquiries : average monthly wage of head of household . .	71·78	77·49	85·29
Current statistics : average monthly wage :			
Same districts as above . .	—	64·64	69·02
Whole of Russia . . .	52·93	59·83	65·14

Relation of Wages to Total Family Income

The incomes of Russian workers differ from those of industrial workers in other European countries in many respects. Wages constitute some four-fifths of the Russian worker's income, the remainder being obtained from other sources, such as the sale of goods, loans, insurance benefits, etc., which are described below.

The percentage of the total family income represented by the wages earned by the head of the household in his chief occupation varied as follows from 1922 to 1927 : *

Year				Per cent.
1922	.	.	.	64–73
1923	.	.	.	72·5
1924	.	.	.	72·5
1925	.	.	.	73·3
1926	.	.	.	79·0
1927	.	.	.	80·4

* *Ibid.*

The wages of other members of the family as well as the subsidiary earnings of the head of the household raised the percentage represented by family earnings to 80—88 per cent., but the general result remains the same : wages in Russia on the whole constitute four-fifths of the income, and one-fifth, on the average, has to be provided from other sources.

These other sources of income are insurance and other benefits paid by the State, trade unions, and other institutions, the sale and pawning of household belongings and other goods, credits and loans, subletting rooms and " corners," income derived from boarders, etc.

Among these sources of income, insurance and other benefits paid by the State and the trade unions form a more or less stable item of income, constituting on an average 4 per cent. of the total.

Credits, loans, and pawning are the next item of importance ; they constituted, on the average, in 1925 and 1926 more than 5 per cent. of the total income, though in 1927 they are shown as only 1 per cent.*

The subletting of rooms and " corners " and income derived from boarders do not form a large item in the income of a worker's family, but they seem to be increasing. The sale of goods, on the contrary, shows a tendency to diminish ; it now

---

* It should be pointed out that these percentages represent only the balance ; *i.e.*, the difference between the sums borrowed and the sums repaid during the month covered by the enquiry. In 1927, for instance, the total (average) loans were 8·71 roubles, as against 7.42 roubles in 1926, and the repayments were 8.12 and 6.76 roubles respectively. These repayments were made by drawing on savings. While the repayment of loans means an improvement in the state of the finances of a worker's family, the fact of drawing on their savings denotes on the contrary a reduction in their resources.

If the absolute value of loans is taken, it will be found that they represented 6·6 per cent. of the total receipts of a worker's family in 1926 and 7·2 per cent. in 1927.

plays a much smaller part than in previous years, when it was an important item of income, as subsidies and wages were paid in kind instead of in cash, and goods so obtained were sold for cash in the market.

The sources of the total income of a worker's family from 1925 to 1927 (averages for the Moscow, Leningrad, Ural, and Donbas regions) are shown in the following table.

AVERAGE MONTHLY INCOME FROM VARIOUS SOURCES
OF A WORKER'S FAMILY, 1925–27 [1]

Source.	Amount (chervonets roubles)			Per cent.		
	1925	1926	1927	1925	1926	1927
Wages from chief occupation of head of household and members of the family . . .	79·59	85·66	93·42	81·3	82·5	88·1
Subsidiary wages . .	0·75	0·90	1·63	0·7	0·8	1·5
Social insurance, unemployment and other benefits.	4·07	4·43	4·20	4·2	4·2	4·1
Sale of own produce .	2·21	1·64	1·62	2·3	1·8	1·5
Sale of property . .	0·95	0·70	0·66	1·0	0·7	0·6
Loans, credit, and pawning	5·63	5·58	1·08	5·7	5·4	1·0
Subletting rooms, boarders	0·48	0·68	0·75	0·4	0·6	0·7
Savings and investments .	1·44	1·66	1·63	1·5	1·6	1·5
Other items . . .	2·78	2·65	1·21	2·9	2·6	1·0
Total . .	97·90	103·90	106·20	100·0	100·0	100·0

[1] *Statistical Review*, 1927, No. 5 ; 1928, No. 5.

EXPENDITURE

The expenditure of a worker's family is also the subject of detailed investigation. The housewife, for instance, is asked not only about the expenditure on clothes, but about the materials used in mending them, sewing needles, reels of cotton, etc. Similarly expenditure on education is taken to include not only fees paid, but also money spent on books, library fees, newspapers and periodicals, stationery, theatres, cinemas, lectures, and all kinds of amusement.

The total expenditure of a worker's family from 1925 to 1927 (averages for the Moscow, Leningrad, Ural, and Donbas regions) is shown in the following table.

AVERAGE MONTHLY EXPENDITURE OF A WORKER'S FAMILY, 1925–27 [1]

Item	Amount (chervonets roubles)			Per cent.		
	1925	1926	1927	1925	1926	1927
Food	43·38	46·89	48·23	44·5	46·0	45·4
Clothing	22·52	19·64	22·57	23·1	19·3	21·3
Rent	5·58	6·84	8·20	5·7	6·7	7·7
Fuel and lighting . .	6·71	7·06	7·05	6·8	6·9	6·6
Furniture . . .	2·82	2·75	2·97	2·9	2·7	2·8
Hygiene and medical services . . .	0·86	0·95	1·04	0·9	0·9	1·0
Drink and tobacco . .	3·45	4·00	4·95	3·5	3·9	4·7
Education, social and political expenses . .	3·87	4·85	4·72	4·0	4·8	4·4
Other items . . .	8·36	9·02	6·47	8·6	8·8	6·1
Total . .	97·55	102·00	106·20	100·0	100·0	100·0

[1] *Statistical Review*, 1927, No. 5 ; 1928, No. 5.

Food

The Russian worker's family thus spends nearly half its total income on food. The author of an article on family budgets in the *Statistical Review*, arrives at the conclusion that the consumption of Russian workers during the last few years is marked by a tendency to eat more meat, butter, eggs, and milk, and less vegetables, potatoes, and bread.*

The following table shows the consumption of the chief items of food during the month of the enquiry in each of the three years 1925–27.

* *Statistical Review*, 1928, No. 5, p. 51.

AVERAGE MONTHLY CONSUMPTION OF FOOD PER ADULT
IN 1925–27 [1]

Item	1925	1926	1927
	Kg.	Kg.	Kg.
Bread and flour . .	20·238	20·481	19·891
Buckwheat . .	1·208	1·039	1·114
Potatoes . . .	14·055	14·399	12·290
Vegetables . .	5·966	5·614	6·118
Meat . . .	6·708	6·905	7·092
Fish	1·016	1·103	1·053
Milk . . .	6·284	6·081	6·777
Butter . . .	0·802	0·802	0·847
Eggs . . .	0·198	0·180	0·362
Sugar . . .	1·343	1·536	1·724
Tea	0·030	0·033	0·031

[1] *Statistical Review*, 1927, No. 5 ; 1928, No. 5.

1927 may have been an exceptional year ; vegetables
were consumed in larger quantities than in the two
previous years ; the quantities of other items had
not increased to any great extent, and prices for
potatoes in 1927 were 17·6 per cent. higher than in
1926 ; the diminution of consumption of potatoes
may therefore be due entirely to their high price
(6 gold kopeks instead of 5 gold kopeks per kilogram).

Clothing

Clothing is the next most important item of
expenditure.

The consumption of clothing increased in quantity
between November 1926 and November 1927.

The family budget investigators point out that the
high prices and scarcity of ready-made clothing
oblige the workers to buy material. Furthermore,
the rise in the prices of stuffs of better quality (cloth)
has reduced their consumption, while the purchases
of cheaper stuffs have on the contrary increased.

The quantity of cloth purchased per head fell from 0·018 metre in November 1926 to 0·014 metre in November 1927, a reduction of 22·2 per cent. The amount of cotton goods purchased, however, rose from 1·176 to 1·353 metres. During the period in question, in fact, the price of cotton goods fell by 10·5 per cent., while cloth rose by 14 per cent. and other woollen goods by 34 per cent. on the average.

It is also to be noted that purchases made in one particular month are affected by market conditions ; purchases of clothing in particular are seasonal and are very irregular.*

Fuel

The average expenditure on fuel during 1925–27 was about 7 per cent. of the total. The same percentage is found also in the pre-war budget enquiries (7·2 per cent. for St. Petersburg in 1908), but this does not indicate that conditions, in so far as fuel is concerned, have remained identical ; the housing accommodation for workers is now quite different from that of pre-war times, and the supply of fuel is also different. The only tendency that can be observed in the budget enquiries is that coal is rising in price, and paraffin as a fuel is therefore becoming more and more popular.

Rent

In the first years of the Revolution, Russian workers were living rent free ; subsequently, in the first years of the New Economic Policy, rent used to absorb only from 1·5 to 3 per cent. of income. During 1925–27, the budget enquiries show a constant rise of expenditure on rent ; in 1925 it represented 5·7 per cent. of the whole family income, in 1926 6·7 per cent., and in 1927 7·7 per cent. At the

* *Idem*, 1928, No. 5, p. 54.

same time, housing conditions were becoming more difficult for Russian workers ; in 1925, in the four regions where the budget enquiries were made, the average space per person was 5·14 square metres ; in 1926 it fell to 5·01 square metres ; in 1927 it rose to 5·04 square metres, but more had to be paid per square metre of lodging. In 1925 the Moscow workers were paying 25 kopeks per square metre ; in 1926 they already had to pay 54 kopeks ; in Leningrad the rates were 18 and 22 kopeks respectively. The average for all four regions was 22 kopeks in 1926 and 27 kopeks in 1927.*

Tobacco and Drink

In pre-war times the Russian worker used to spend 6 per cent. of his income on tobacco and drink.† Now (according to the latest budget enquiry) he spends 5 per cent.

According to recent data, the average annual consumption of alcohol has increased as follows (bottles per member of a worker's family) : ‡

Region	1925	1926	1927
Capital cities . . .	11·96	17·07	18·45
Other towns of R. S. F. S. R.	3·35	6·83	10·35
Ukraine	4·84	10·67	12·00
All U. S. S. R. . . .	5·37	9·64	12·27

Hygiene and Medical Services

This item of expenditure is much lower than in pre-war budgets owing to the privileges given in Soviet Russia to the working classes, which make access to medical services much easier and cheaper.

* *Idem,* 1927, No. 5, p. 41 ; 1928, No. 5, p. 49.
† Bulletin of the Departmental Office of Statistics (Moscow), 1924, No. 87, p. 70.
‡ *Economicheskoe Obozrenie* (*Economic Review*), 1928, No. 11, p. 150.

Education, Social and Political Expenses

This expenditure includes membership fees to trade unions and political and social subscriptions. The *Statistical Review* states that the higher percentage of this item in 1926 was due to the subscription for the support of British miners.*

In conclusion some information may be given as to the sources from which Russian workers buy their food and other necessaries. The following interesting table is given by the *Statistical Review*.†

PERCENTAGES OF FOOD, FUEL, AND CLOTHING PURCHASED BY RUSSIAN WORKERS FROM VARIOUS SOURCES, 1926 AND 1927 [1]

Item and period [a]	Private trade	Co-operative societies	State stores	Various
Food :				
1926 . . .	40·6	52·5	2·7	4·2
1927 . . .	29·9	64·5	1·3	4·3
Fuel and light :				
1926 . . .	27·1	16·6	15·5	40·8
1927 . . .	20·9	19·0	16·8	43·3
Clothing and boots :				
1926 . . .	37·7	49·7	11·5	1·1
1927 . . .	26·4	60·3	11·5	1·8
Total				
1926 . .	38·3	49·8	6·6	5·3
1927 . .	27·5	60·8	6·2	5·5

[1] *Statistical Review*, 1928, No. 5, p. 53.
[a] November of each year.

In 1927 Russian workers made 60·8 per cent. of

* *Statistical Review*, 1928, No. 5, p. 55.
† The official figures furnished by the co-operative societies were contested by the delegates to the last (Eighth) Congress of Trade Unions in December, 1928. The delegates considered that as regards foodstuffs in particular the co-operative societies only supply the workers with 20–25 per cent. of the total. (*Trud* (*Labour*), December 22nd, 1928.)

their purchases from co-operative stores, 27·5 per cent. from private traders, and 6·2 per cent. from the State stores. The proportion in the preceding year had been as follows : 49·8 from co-operative stores, 38·3 per cent. from private traders, and 6·6 per cent. from the State stores.*

This report was prepared in 1929, and the data concerning workers' family budgets related to the period of the New Economic Policy prior to the First Five-Year-Plan. Since the introduction of the Plan, or soon after, the publication of enquiries into workers' budgets has been discontinued and the Central Statistical Bureau has been abolished. It would, therefore, be impossible now to make comparison along the same lines.

There is plenty of information concerning the increase of nominal wages under the Five-Year-Plan (1928–33) in the official statistics of the U.S.S.R. (the only statistics available). But there is very little information as to the real wages of workers, their actual expenditure and the prices of commodities consumed.†

Some of the economists, visitors to Russia and organisations like the International Labour Office of the League of Nations, the Amsterdam World Social-Economic Congress, etc., have made attempts to compare the present standard of life of Russian workers with that at previous periods, as well as with

---

* In 1933 the Co-operative Societies were carrying out 46·1 per cent. of the total retail trade in Soviet Russia, and the State (*Gostorg*) 32·7 per cent. The remaining 21·2 per cent. was done by the O.W.S. (Organisations for Workers' Supply), by various co-operative societies, and other organisations. (" The Consumers' Co-operation in the U.S.S.R. in 1929–33." Moscow, 1934, p. 49.)

† In the Materials to the Report of the Narkomtrud to the Ninth All-Union Congress of Trade Unions, for instance, we do not find any references to the expenditure of workers. The increase of nominal average wages is given there as follows :

workers' earnings abroad. But all these attempts, in spite of their great value and interest, are very incomplete and somewhat contradictory when compared with each other.

Official Soviet publications naturally record a great increase of wages and a constantly rising standard of life for all workers engaged in industry and agriculture, but the extent of this rise and its value cannot be verified and tested at present owing to the absence of impartial information as to prices and consumption.

YEARLY AVERAGE WAGES IN ROUBLES SINCE 1928

	1928	1929	1930	1931	Increase since 1928
					per cent.
Census industry .	870	958	1,003	1,167	34·1
Building industry .	996	1,063	1,102	1,280	28·5
Railways . .	859	908	1,032	1,142	33

The monthly nominal average wages for the coal-mining industry are given in the Report as follows : in 1928, 63.27 roubles ; in 1929, 68.81 ; in 1930, 76.47 ; in 1931, 94.47. This gives an increase of the nominal average wage since 1928 of 49·3 per cent. ("Labour in the U.S.S.R." Moscow, 1932, pp. 23–25.)

THE CO-OPERATIVE MOVEMENT
IN RUSSIA*

THE co-operative movement in Russia is very interesting. But if we wish to understand it, we must acquaint ourselves with the background in which this movement was developing. We must remember that Russia has always been—and still is —a vast agricultural country. Its population on the eve of the last War was over 150 millions, of whom 80 millions were peasants. There were only three millions of industrial workers in Russia and from 12 to 15 millions of wage-earners.

The population of Russia from the very beginnings of the Russian Empire has learned to rely on a system of local government. The Mir—a meeting of village elders—was always the first authority, the decisions of which were final for the whole village. All the central Government's officials were considered to be an unavoidable evil, sent to the village for fiscal purposes only. The writings of the best Russian authors always reveal the peasants' love of freedom and self-determination. The population of Russia was kept for a long time in a servile position by means of terror, reprisals and severe punishment. The peasants could not liberate themselves, for they, being illiterate and uneducated, had no conception of national unity : their ideas did not go beyond their own district. The country was vast, the means of communication were primitive and there was no

* A lecture delivered by the present writer at the Summer School of the Co-operative Party at Cober Hill, Cloughton, near Scarborough, in September 1927.

possibility of creating a united front of all those who were oppressed.

Such was the background in which the Russian co-operative societies developed ; the social and economic conditions were no doubt favourable to their growth. Poor, oppressed, illiterate and robbed by everyone who was not too lazy to rob—the Russian peasants could not help welcoming any idea which showed them the way to self-help, self-determination and self-defence against middlemen and local rich storekeepers, who also were very often owners of the village inn (*kulaks*).

The first attempts to build a co-operative movement in Russia occurred in the early 'sixties of the nineteenth century, when the ideas of Robert Owen and Charles Fourier were introduced to the Russian people by Dobrolubov, Chernyshevsky and other writers. The co-operative ideas of Schultze, from Delitch, in Germany, also greatly influenced our co-operative movement. The first consumers' societies were started in the 'sixties in Riga, Reval and St. Petersburg, and gradually permeated the country. Credit societies were advocated by the pioneer of our co-operative movement, B. Louginin, who organised the first credit association near Kostroma in Central Russia. Russian Zemstvos (county councils), established in 1864, helped the Russian peasants by means of small credit operations, and assisted them in acquiring cattle, simple agricultural machinery and fertilisers.

But all the endeavours of well-meaning educated people and of the local government were hampered by the central Government, which was opposed to the peasants taking an active share in the economic and political life of the country. Trade unions and consumers' co-operative societies were prohibited ;

all attempts to help the working classes in their education or even to collect statistical information on the life of the labouring people were considered a political crime.

The co-operative movement in Russia began to develop more or less normally after the Revolution of 1905, and could only then be described as a genuine people's movement.*

The rapidity with which the movement grew can be seen from the following table :

Numbers of	1905	1914	January 1st, 1917
Savings Banks and Credit establishments . .	1,434	12,751	16,057
Consumers' Co-operative Societies	1,000	10,080	20,000
Agricultural Co-operative Societies	1,275	5,000	6,000
Artels and Dairy Co-operative Societies	2,000	3,000	4,000
Total . . .	5,709	30,831	46,057

Sixty per cent. of the consumers' co-operative societies were situated in the countryside, close to the large industrial centres, and in the villages. The main types of these rural societies were :

(*a*) The factory co-operative stores which united workers of the factory only and which did not admit members from outside.

(*b*) The home industry co-operative stores, which served the members of a certain craft.

(*c*) The agricultural consumers' societies which united peasants working on the land.

(*d*) The village co-operative stores, which united all inhabitants of a village.

* S. Petrovich, " The Consumers' Co-operative Societies in Russia, " in the *Help Worker*. Moscow, 1907, p. 52.

Some of these societies were connected with the *Centrosoyus* (the equivalent of the British Co-operative Wholesale Society).

The goods supplied by the consumers' co-operative societies were usually the necessaries of life. The average value of goods sold in their stores equalled to £1,000 sterling per annum, though some of the large stores sold as much as £10,000 or even £40,000 sterling worth of goods a year.

The average membership was between 100 to 200. Profits were shared among members in the usual manner, and varied from 5 to 10 per cent. on each share. Premiums on goods purchased varied from ½ to 10 per cent.

Agricultural co-operative societies and *artels* played an important part in the economic life of Russia. An *artel* is the oldest type of co-operative effort, and was created by the peasants themselves. It was described by the Russian Law as " an association formed to carry out specified units of work or carry on certain industries, or render personal services on the joint responsibility of the members of the *artel* and for their joint account." But it was more than merely a producer's co-operative society, for their purchases of material and of foodstuffs and of various necessaries were also carried on on co-operative lines.

We find *artels* all over Russia ; they were closely connected with the Russian home industry, in which about 20 millions of the population were engaged, making toys, furniture, carving and painting woodwork, etc. There were also *artels* of builders and painters, agricultural societies working on the land, *artels* of flax-growers, *artels* engaged in the marketing of eggs and other farm produce. The *artels* did not possess much capital, the membership was limited, but all members were picked men, accustomed to work with each other and obedient to the strict discipline of their organisation. The majority of *artels* produced their goods for sale in the open market, but they were usually open to orders and commissions from industrial firms, in which case the latter supplied them with materials and a certain amount of capital.

The credit associations in Russia were of two types : credit societies and savings associations. The latter were popular in the Baltic provinces and in Poland, where the peasants were better off and were able to save more and to invest more of their money. The credit societies did not depend much for their capital upon the subscriptions of their members—for the initial capital was provided by the State Bank. Their operations were mainly confined to the acceptance of deposits and to the granting of credits to members, for the purpose of purchasing agricultural machinery, livestock, seeds and raw materials.

All Russian consumers' credit and agricultural societies were united into local unions, and some of them were affiliated to one of the two existing central organisations—the *Centrosoyus* and the People's Bank in Moscow.

The *Centrosoyus* was created in 1898 on the initiative of eighteen consumers' societies. Within a few years it had grown into a very powerful organisation. In 1910 it united 400 societies with a turnover of £220,000 sterling. In 1915 there were already 1,700 societies with a turnover of £2,200,000. Thus, in five years, the turnover had increased tenfold. In 1916 the turnover had reached £4,500,000 during the first eight months of the year.

The People's Bank (The Moscow Narodny Bank) was created in 1911 with a capital of £100,000, divided into shares of £25 each ; 85 per cent. of these shares were immediately taken up by the co-operative societies, and the Bank began operations in 1912. The object of the Bank was to supply co-operative societies with credit and to facilitate their business transactions. The activities of the Bank developed very rapidly, and it opened several branches in the country and abroad. Its turnover in 1916 had reached the figure of £6,000,000 sterling.

The World War naturally interfered with the normal work of the co-operative societies, but in spite of it, they did their duty nobly. At a time when the Government showed every sign of complete degeneration, the Russian town and county councils and the co-operative organisations took upon themselves the burden of maintaining the economic life of the country, which was destroyed by the War and by the Civil War.

The exact figure of actual members of distributive co-operative societies in Russia on December 31st, 1918, according to the Report to the International Congress of Co-operative Societies in Paris in 1919, stood at 10,269,757 ; this refers to the number of heads of families only and counting each family as consisting of five persons, we realise that about 60 million persons, or about a third of the population of pre-war Russia, relied on co-operatives for their provisioning with prime necessities. About 80 per cent. of the membership of the movement was formed of peasants. The above-mentioned 10 million persons were organised in approximately 25,000 individual co-operative societies, of which twenty societies counted over 10,000 members each, while the Moscow distributive store " Kooperatsia " counted over 210,000 members. These distributive societies were organised into 500 local unions ; local unions were again united in the All-Russian Central Union of

Consumers' Societies—the *Centrosoyus*. The capital of the Central Union amounted to 100 million roubles (£10,000,000 sterling) while the total turnover during 1918 reached 1,000 million roubles (£100,000,000 sterling).

The industrial co-operative societies were also growing in numbers and importance. The yearly output of the undertakings owned by the All-Russian Central Union of Consumers' Societies represented commodities valued at 150 million roubles (£15,000,000 sterling).*

Such was the position of the Russian co-operative movement before the Revolution of 1917 and for two years after it, when it was rebuilt entirely on quite new lines and principles. The Revolution of 1917 had given great hopes to the Russian co-operative organisations, and during that year they were, as we have already mentioned—together with the town and county councils—the sole agents for the supply and distribution of food and other necessaries among the rural and urban population. In October of the same year, when the Bolsheviks came to power, the co-operatives still enjoyed their freedom. Free co-operative societies existed in Russia until the March of 1920, when every adult person in Russia was compelled by law to become a member of a local distributive co-operative society ; the shareholdings of individual members were returned to them and the capital of the co-operative societies became nationalised.†

According to the authoritative opinion of a well-known Russian co-operator : " The last remnants of co-operation were destroyed by the Decrees of the 27th January and of the 19th of April of 1920. All

---

* *The Russian Co-operator.* London, 1919, Vol. 3, No. 8.
† *The Russian Co-operator.* London, 1920, Vol. 4, No. 7.

co-operative organisations were welded into a consumers' commune and subordinated to it. These united communes, together with their departmental and central organisations constituted the State distributive machine, maintained by government grants, and indistinguishable from the other organs of the Government. But notwithstanding all this, they were still called *Centrosoyus*, or the All-Russian Union of Consumers' Societies. A similar description of the position of co-operative societies is to be found in the investigation published by the International Labour Office : " At the beginning of 1920 the consumers' co-operative organisation underwent the following changes :

" 1. The old consumers' societies, whether general or industrial, were converted into united consumers' communities embracing all the consumers' organisations.

" 2. All workers were compelled to join the consumers' communities, without payment of fees.

" 3. All so-called bourgeois were excluded from the consumers' communities.

" 4. The entire structure of the consumers' organisation was remodelled.

" 5. The consumers' communities were made government bodies dependent on the Commissariat of Supply. All officials of these communities became Soviet officials.

" 6. All the old leaders of the consumers' co-operatives were turned out and replaced by Communists, both at the central headquarters and in the provinces." *

* " The Co-operative Movement in Russia." Geneva, 1925, p. 35. In April 1921 *The Russian Co-operator*, an official journal of the *Centrosoyus*, published in London the following Declaration of the Russian Co-operators :

" 1. The Soviet Government does in no case allow individuals to unite freely for economic purposes.

" 2. The commune of consumers, which is compulsorily formed by the Soviet Government, is in its work confined to distribution.

" 3. The right to elect officers exists only on paper. Actually the elections in the communes are taking place under such conditions that there can be no talk of free self-government of the communes, even within the limits of their rights.

The Soviet Government, after the introduction of the New Economic Policy (N.E.P.) in 1921, gave more freedom to the co-operatives in so far as their business transactions were concerned ; gradually, also, it permitted them to become less centralised. But the principle of compulsory membership of co-operative societies was still left in force, and only on May 20th, 1924, a decree was issued, according to which " the right to found consumers' societies is confined to citizens of the Soviet Union who possess electoral rights under the Soviet Constitution. All such citizens are free to join or to resign from a co-operative society ; citizens can only become members of a consumers' society at their own express wish. They may leave such a society at will. They may also be expelled in accordance with the regulations (Section 2 of the Decree). Consumers' Societies are entitled to sell their goods to the public (Section 4). The new Decree lays down that the purchase of shares is compulsory and not optional as under the Decree of April 7th, 1921. To facilitate the entry of poor citizens, the entrance fee was fixed at 50 gold kopeks (one shilling) and the amount of shares at five gold roubles (10 shillings). Once the entrance fee was paid, a citizen became a member of the co-operative society. The share might be paid up in instalments (Section 7). There is no limit to the number of

" 4. The unions of communes are formed, not by the free will and according to the desires and aims of the co-operators, but, in accordance with Soviet decrees.

" 5. The provincial unions also have no free choice for electing the executive bodies.

" 6. Under these circumstances, the Centrosoyus must be considered as a compulsory state organisation, at the head of which stand almost exclusively officials of the Soviet.

" 7. The whole variegated and many-sided valuable organisation of co-operative education and co-operative propaganda has been destroyed. If a co-operative journal remained it was handed over to the Communist party."

shares held by one member, but no special privileges accrue to the holder of several shares (Note to Section 7). The transfer of shares is prohibited (Section 8). A society may not be registered unless it has at least thirty members ; in certain places this minimum may be raised."*

Having described briefly the development of the Russian co-operative movement, we must say a few words about the principles on which the Soviet Government began to build consumers' co-operatives after the New Economic Policy.

" The principal task of consumers' co-operation is to socialise the process of the circulation of commodities and the organisation of the home market." The co-operative societies in Russia " under the Soviet system discard their isolated group character . . . they obtain their goods from the State industries, use the State transport facilities, and a large part of their trading capital consists of State Credits." " The Communist party carries on a good deal of work in connection with the activities of the co-operative movement and exercise considerable influence upon co-operative life."

" The Communist party imposes upon all its members the obligation of taking an active part in the co-operative movement." " Under Soviet conditions the policy of reducing prices takes the place of the old Rochdale principle of trading at average market prices."† These few quotations illustrate how different are these principles to those accepted by the International Co-operative Congresses.

* " The Co-operative Movement in Soviet Russia." International Labour Office. Geneva, 1925, p. 281.

† N. Popoff. " Consumers' Co-operation in the U.S.S.R." London, 1927, p. 8, etc.

STATISTICAL SUPPLEMENT
AND DOCUMENTS

APPENDIX I

THE REGULATION OF 1741

THIS Regulation instructed the owners of the factories

(a) To take precautions against fire, to make provision for adequate lighting and heating and to provide sufficient space for each loom.

(b) To provide adequate supplies of raw materials, so that no time should be lost by the workers ; if shortage of material occurred, the owners were obliged to pay a certain minimum wage to the workers.

(c) To build workers' barracks near the factory ; the cost of construction was gradually to be deducted from wages.

(d) To provide a hospital in the barracks.

(e) To introduce a scale of wages for all the workers in the factory.

(f) Wages were to be paid weekly ; 25 per cent. of all wages were to be retained as a deposit to cover possible damage to the owners' property. At the end of each month the balance of the deposit which remained after deduction of fines was to be paid to the workers.

(g) All fines went to constitute a special fund, from which the claims of owners for damage done were to be paid. The balance of the fund was to be used for the maintenance of factory hospitals and as awards to workers for the best work done. Maximum fines were fixed by the Regulation and a progressive scale was worked out for repeated offences.

(h) A uniform dress was to be provided for all workers ; and the cost of this was to be covered by deductions from wages.

Two interesting paragraphs in the Regulation must also be mentioned here. In the first of them it was said that " The wives and daughters of workers may only be employed in factories if they express the wish to work there, and their wages must be the same as those paid to men." This applied, however, only to " freely-hired " workers and to workers attached to factories. The second paragraph of the Regulation warned the owners against the use of the *knut* (whip) and against sending workers to hard labour in Siberia " where they run the danger of losing their skill " (A. Bykov, " Factory Legislation, etc.," p. 133).

APPENDIX II

NUMBER OF WORKERS, WAGES AND PRICES IN RUSSIA IN THE FIRST HALF OF THE NINETEENTH CENTURY *

I. NUMBER OF WORKERS

IN 1804 there were in Russia, excluding mines, 2,423 factories with 95,202 workers ; of these, 45,625, or 48 per cent., were hired labourers. In 1814 the number of factories had increased to 3,731 with 169,530 workers. In 1825 there were already 5,261 factories with 210,568 workers, 54 per cent. of them being hired labourers. The distribution of workers according to the different branches of industry was as follows :—

NUMBER OF WORKERS IN " POSSESSIONAL " AND " VOTCHINI " FACTORIES (excluding mines, wine, and beer distilleries, and factories in Finland and Poland) IN 1825

Branches of industry	Total number of workers	Of these	
		Votchini	Possessional and bought
Woollen . . .	63,603	38,583	13,315
Cotton . . .	47,021	247	2,239
Linen . . .	26,832	1,483	6,629
Silk	10,204	658	1,065
Paper making . .	8,272	3,350	2,903
Cutlery and tools (including needles and pins) . . .	22,440	14,820	2,650
Rope making . .	2,503	167	33
Leather . . .	8,001	539	2
Total . .	210568	66,725	29,328

This table shows the increase of " votchini" workers as compared with the " possessional," which was due, to a great extent, to the introduction of the *obrok* system.

* Compare B. B. Glinsky, " The History of the Russian Factory " in the *Historical Review.* St. Petersburg, 1898, Vol. V., 74, p. 267 ; V. T. Pecheta, in the " National War 1812-1912." Moscow, 1911, Vol. VII., p. 248 ; A. Bykov, *op. cit.*, p. 136 ; M. Tugan-Baranovsky, *op. cit.*, Ed. 1922, p. 73, etc.

II. Wages and Prices

Data as to wages at the beginning of the nineteenth century are very scarce and often very contradictory. The following table gives an idea of the average wages of "possessional" workers in the textile industry :—

Average Monthly Wages in 1803 of "Possessional" Workers in the Textile Industry

Categories of workers	Woollen industry (Moscow Province)	Silk industry (Moscow and Yaroslavl Province)	Linen industry (Yaroslavl Province)
	(In paper roubles—assignations)		
Foreman . .	7.00	4.00–10.00	6 50–8.90
Journeymen .	—	4.50	3.50–4.00
Weavers :			
Men . .	3.00–6.60	3.75–7.80	4.15
Women .	2.60	—	2.52
Apprentice .	—	4.50–5.00	1.63
Others . .	2.50–3.50	1.38–4.50	1.44–4.90

The average nominal wage, according to this computation, was 4 paper roubles. Taking into consideration the price of bread and calculating the wages on the gold rouble, this would come approximately to 5.64 roubles per month. On this money wage the Russian textile worker could hardly exist if he did not receive in addition a wage in kind : fuel and building materials for the house, benefits for the children and for members of the family incapable of working. His government taxes were usually paid by the factory owner and, in the majority of cases, they were not deducted afterwards from the wages. Flour was usually sold to the workmen from the factory stores at cost price. But even these additional benefits did not assure a decent standard of living, and we notice that strikes were often declared on the ground of low wages and unfairness in the distribution of benefits.

During the first half of the nineteenth century wages, owing to the boom in the Russian textile industry, rose considerably. Money wages in the silk factory at Fryanovo, near Moscow, for instance, rose between 1802 and 1820 by 92 to 206 per cent. In the factory at Kupavna (each of these factories employed over 1,000 workers) money wages trebled. As the price of bread rose over the same period by 139 per cent., the average real wage increase was 25 per cent. In Ivanovo-Voznessensk, near Moscow, where the cotton industry in its first stage enjoyed a complete monopoly, owners' profits were as high as 500 per cent. Money wages here were also very high, but towards the middle of the century the average earnings of these workers came down to the level of all other textile workers.*

AVERAGE WAGES IN THE MINING AREA OF URAL MOUNTAINS AT THE BEGINNING OF THE EIGHTEENTH CENTURY AND IN 1855–60

Categories of workers	In roubles per annum Money wages plus wages in kind	
	At the beginning of Eighteenth century	1855–60
Foreman :		
Single . . .	24 to 36	46 to 82
Married . . .	24 to 36	66 to 102
Skilled labourers :		
Single . . .	18	28
Married . . .	18	48
Unskilled labourers :		
Single . . .	12	20
Married . . .	12	40

" The general rise in wages during a century and a half," says K. Pazhitnov, " was from 55 to 66 per cent. for the single worker and from 92 to 128 per cent. for the single master : for the married worker from 166 to 233 per cent ; and for the married master from 175 to 183 per cent." The price of bread trebled during this period, and prices of other necessities showed an even greater increase. The conditions of workers' lives, therefore, did not improve very much, especially as wages in kind consisted of bread and flour only

* Tugan-Baranovsky, *op. cit.*, ed. 1922, p. 146.

and the other necessities had to be bought out of money wages.*

The wages of workers employed in the Siberian gold mines, and the conditions of work there, were even worse. The workman received only from 60 to 70 per cent. of his wages in money, the remaining 30 to 40 per cent. being paid in kind from the stores attached to the mines. The majority of the workmen were usually in debt to the stores, which charged them exorbitant prices : 11 per cent. above the market price for tea, 21 per cent. for tobacco and from 28 to 33 per cent. for flour. Manufactured goods brought from the European part of Russia were priced at 50 per cent., and even more, above their market prices.

The average money wage in the gold mines in the middle of the nineteenth century was 56 to 57 silver roubles per year.† This could hardly cover the advance of money which each worker used to get before he arrived in the mines, which were sometimes situated 1,000 miles from his home. In order to provide himself and his family with bare necessities, he would have to earn, according to N. Flerovsky, at least 133 roubles.‡

* K. Pazhitnov, *Archives*, Vol. III., p. 15.

† V. Semevsky, " Goldminers in Siberia." St. Petersburg, 1898, Vol. I., p. 221, etc.

‡ N. Flerovsky, " The Working Class in Russia." St. Petersburg, 1869, p. 281, etc.

APPENDIX III

RULES OF EMPLOYMENT OF PERSONS
FREELY-HIRED, 1857 *
(SUMMARY)

" Article 100. Freely-hired people may be engaged for work according to the general rules of employment (March, 1762).

" Article 101. Registration of these people in the trade corporations is not required.

" Article 102. Everybody who has a passport may apply for work for the term during which the passport is valid (1835).

" Article 103. Nobody has the right to leave the factory or to ask for increased wages before the end of the agreement. The Government authorities and noblemen who issued passports have no right to call anybody away from the factory (except in the case of criminal prosecution or military service).

" Article 104. The owner of a factory may dismiss his employee in case of disobedience or of non-fulfilment of his duties by giving him two weeks' notice.

" Article 105. Owners of factories are liable to fines (according to Article 1868 of the Penal Code) if they reduce wages before the expiration of an agreement, or insist on the acceptance of wages in kind.

" Article 106. The owner of a factory has no right to employ persons without passport.

" Article 107. Owners of factories are at liberty to conclude either a written agreement with workers and masters, or to keep wage sheets on which the conditions of work must be entered together with an indication of the monthly or daily wages. Apart from the above, owners are obliged to keep a special book in which payments to workers must be entered.

* " Law Code of the Russian Empire." St. Petersburg, 1857, Vol. XI., p. 11, Div. IV., Arts. 100–114.

" Article 108. The factory rules have to be affixed to the walls of the workshops.

" Article 109. The rules, wage sheets and books are accepted by the Courts as evidence in case of a claim.

" Article 110. Persons disclosing secrets of production are liable to a penalty according to Article 1864 of the Penal Code.

" Article 111. If an " artel " or group of workers shows evident disobedience to the owner of a factory or his representative, they are liable to penalties under Article 1865 of the Penal Code.

" Article 112. Those who are responsible for a strike, declared before the termination of an agreement, with the object of inducing the owners to raise wages, are liable to punishment according to Article 1866 of the Penal Code.

" Article 113. Passports may be prolonged with the consent of both parties.

" Article 114. The owner of a factory has no power to retain the passport of a worker if he leaves him."

The general rules of employment, to which Article 100 referred, defined the categories of persons who were debarred from seeking employment :—

(a) Children without the consent of their parents or guardians.

(b) Wives without the consent of their husbands.

(c) Bonded persons without passports from their owners (Article 2202).

The other paragraphs of these general rules dealt with certain restrictions of noblemen's rights to send their bondsmen for employment, prescribed a certain form for agreements and gave general advice for both parties as to how to behave and how to treat persons in employment.*

" Possessional " workers or attached to factories, or bought, were also mentioned in the Russian Law Code of 1857, and several provisions were devoted to them, such as the following :—†

" Article 88. Workers attached to factories, or bought, are the property of the factory itself, but not of the tenant

* " Law Code of the Russian Empire." St. Petersburg, 1857, Vol. X., p. 1, Div. IV., Arts. 2202-37.

† Ibid., Vol. XI., p. 11, Book I., Div. II., Ch. IV., Arts. 88-95. See also Vol. VII., Book II., Div. I., Arts. 461-470 ; and Vol. VII., Book III., Div. I., Arts. 1732-49.

of the factory, and remain inseparable from it. They can change their mode of life (that is, their employment) only with the permission of the owner of the factory and ' Collegium of Manufacture.'

" Article 89. All taxes and duties of these workers are payable by the tenants of the factories.

" Article 91. The tenants of ' Possessional ' factories have no right to employ the workers for other than factory work.

" Article 92. They have no right to transfer individual workers or their families to other factories and villages.

" Article 94. Owners of factories have the right to issue passports to their workers (that is, to allow them to work elsewhere)—on condition that this will not affect production and that the taxes for the absent workers are used to assist other workers in case of fire or other misfortune.

" Article 95. Owners have the right in cases of bad behaviour by workers, or of their incapacity, to send them to the Recruiting Officer. In accordance with the Article 463 in Volume VII. of the Law Code, owners of mines are allowed to dismiss, and to issue passports to superfluous workers without replacing them by others (May 20th, 1846)."

Cases of riots and strikes were dealt with by Articles 111 and 112, and those responsible were subject to penalties under Articles 1865 and 1866 of the Penal Code.* According to these Articles, those responsible for a strike must be arrested and detained for from three weeks to three months or from seven days to three weeks. Riots were defined as attacks upon the authorities appointed by the Government, and those responsible for them were subject to penalties enumerated in Articles 296–302 and 306 of the Penal Code :—

" Article 296. Deprivation of all citizens' rights and hard labour in the mines from 15 to 20 years. Corporal punishment—100 strokes, with the imposition of brands.

" Articles 297–298. Deprivation of all citizens' rights, with hard labour from 12 to 15 years, or from 4 to 6 years.

" Article 306. Imprisonment from 6 months to 2 years, or confinement in a lunatic asylum from 2 to 3 years."

* " Law Code of the Russian Empire." Vol. XV., Book II., Div. VIII., Ch. XIV., Arts. 1854–68.

APPENDIX IV

THE "FIRST RUSSIAN LABOUR CODE"

(Summary)

The Law of June 3rd, 1886

" Articles 1–4.   All factory workers must have passports.

" Article 5.   Women and young persons seeking employment need not obtain special permission from their husbands, parents or guardians, if they are in possession of a separate passport.

" Article 6.   Employers have no right to retain workers' passports at the termination of the contract.

" Articles 7–8.   Workers must have wages books or written contracts.

" Article 9.   Contracts can be concluded for a specified period of time, or for a certain amount of work, or for an indefinite period.

" Article 10.   Two weeks' notice must be given by either side on the termination of the contract.

" Article 11.   Wages must not be decreased, and workers have no right to claim a rise in wages, before the termination of contracts.

" Article 12.   Wages must be paid monthly, or every fortnight, and the amount paid must be entered in the wages book.

" Article 13.   Workers have the right to appeal to the Judicial Court if wages are not paid to time.

" Article 14.   It is forbidden to pay wages in kind or in the form of coupons detached from interest-bearing documents (Bonds).

" Article 15.   No deductions are allowed from wages, except in the case of debts to the factory provision stores.

" Article 16.—No charge may be made to workers for medical treatment, use of lights in workshops or the use of tools during work.

" Article 18.   The factory rules must be posted up in the workshops.

" Article 19.   A contract may be terminated before.

expiry, by mutual consent of the parties, or for the following reasons : fire, closing down of the establishment, or deportation of workmen by the police authorities.

" Article 20.   A contract may also be terminated before expiry in the following cases :—

" (a) If workmen are absent from work, without sufficient reason, for more than three days.
" (b) If a worker commits a criminal action.
" (c) In case of bad behaviour and rudeness on the part of a worker.
" (d) In case of infectious disease among the workers.

" Article 21.   The workers have the right to terminate a contract in the following cases :—

" (a) If the employer, or members of the administration, treat them badly, insult them, or beat them.
" (b) If the employer does not comply with the conditions of the contract concerning lodgings and food.
" (c) If conditions of work are dangerous to the health of employees.
" (d) In case of death or illness of one of the members of the family."

Punishment for participation in strikes was laid down in the Law of June 3rd, 1886, as follows :—

" III. 2. For participation in a strike having as its aim to induce the employer to increase wages or to change any other conditions of work before the expiration of a contract, those responsible shall be liable to imprisonment for from 4 to 8 months, if they were the instigators of the strike or encouraged others to take part in it, and to imprisonment for from 2 to 4 months if they only took part in the strike. Those strikers who resume work after the first police warning shall not be liable to any punishment.

" III. 3. Strikers responsible for damage to or the demolition of property belonging to the owners or to any members of the administration shall be liable to imprisonment for from 8 to 16 months, if they incited or inspired the masses or caused work to be interrupted, and to 4 to 8 months' imprisonment if they had a part in the damaging or demolishing of property." *

* " Law Code of the Russian Empire," 3rd edit., Vol. VI., 1886. St. Petersburg, 1888, Arts. 3769, etc., pp. 262 ff.

APPENDIX V

STRIKES DURING THE YEARS 1895–1904 *

NUMBER OF FACTORIES AFFECTED BY DISPUTES AND NUMBER OF WORKPEOPLE INVOLVED, 1895–1904

Year	Number of factories affected by disputes		Number of workers in these enterprises	Number of workers directly involved in disputes	
	Absolute	Per cent. of total		Absolute	Per cent. of total
1895	68	0·36	60,587	31,195	2·01
1896	118	0·62	47,979	29,527	1·94
1897	145	0·75	111,725	59,870	3·99
1898	215	1·13	93,596	43,150	2·87
1899	189	0·99	112,296	97,498	3·83
1900	125	0·73	77,382	29,389	1·73
1901	164	0·96	62,735	32,218	1·89
1902	123	0·72	64,196	36,671	2·15
1903	550	3·21	138,877	86,832	5.10
1904	68	0·40	51,642	24,904	1·46
Total 1,765		—	821,015	431,254	—

The number of disputes varied greatly according to the size of the factories. Factories employing from 20 to 100 workers showed a percentage of disputes ranging from 2·7 to 9·4, whereas in those which employed from 100 to 1,000 workers the percentage varied from 21·5 to 49·9 per year. 60·2 per cent. of the disputes, according to the Report, were " group strikes " affecting several factories in the same industry.

* Statistics of disputes in Russia from 1895 to 1904. Published by the Ministry of Trade and Industry. St. Petersburg. Cited by Koltsov in " The Liberation Movement in Russia at the Beginning of the Twentieth Century." St. Petersburg, 1909, Vol. I., p. 224, etc. The figures in this and the two following tables concern only those factories which were subject to supervision by factory inspectors. They do not include factories situated in Siberia, Asia and the Caucasus, nor State factories and home industries. According to Koltsov, the information given in this table would refer to only about 50 per cent. of all existing factories in Russia, and 70 per cent. of the workers employed.

THE DISTRIBUTION OF DISPUTES AND OF WORKERS
INVOLVED DURING THE YEARS 1895–1904, ACCORDING
TO THE DIFFERENT BRANCHES OF INDUSTRY *

Industry	Number of workers involved	Per cent. of total numbers of workers in the industry	Number of disputes	Per cent. of total number of factories in the industry	Average No. of workers involved in each dispute
Cotton	185,101	47·3	253	29·4	692
Metal	116,937	46·4	336	16·0	348
Other textile	10,736	22·6	44	10·6	244
Hemp, Flax	19,157	19·7	64	12·7	299
Animal products	10,751	19·1	186	13·6	57
Chemicals	11,254	18·1	120	18·8	93
Wool	20,169	14·0	225	21·6	89
Paper	9,154	11·7	136	11·1	67
Minerals	15,791	10·5	129	7·3	122
Woodworking	7,040	8·8	89	5·4	79
Food	23,479	7·7	177	3·1	182
Silk	1,649	5·9	6	2·6	274

From this table it will be seen that the textile and metal
industries were the most affected by disputes : the strikers
involved therein formed a very high percentage of the
workers in those industries, and the average size of each strike
was also the largest.

CAUSES OF STRIKES DURING THE YEARS 1895–1904 †

	No. of disputes	Per cent. of total number of disputes	Number of workers involved	Per cent. of total number of workers involved
A. WAGES :				
Wage increases	754	42·8	98,767	22·9
Wage decreases	128	7·3	61,271	14·5
Mode of payment	189	10·7	48,523	11·2
Total	1,071	60·8	208,561	48·6

* *Ibid.*, p. 226.
† *Ibid.*, pp. 226–227.

CAUSES OF STRIKES DURING THE YEARS 1895-1904—
continued.

	No. of disputes	Per cent. of total number of disputes	Number of workers involved	Per cent. of total number of workers involved
B. HOURS OF LABOUR :				
Shorter hours . .	284	16·1	81,009	18·8
Against prolongation of hours . . .	41	2·3	22,460	5·2
Time table . .	60	3·3	25,889	6·0
Total . .	385	21·7	129,358	30·0
C. WORKING ARRANGE-MENTS, RULES, DIS-CIPLINE, LIVING AC-COMMODATION, FOOD:				
Fines and deductions .	26	1·4	14,727	3·4
Personnel of adminis-tration . . .	77	4·4	40,977	9·5
Lodgings . . .	3	0·2	240	0·05
Food and other condi-tions . . .	25	1·4	2,688	0·6
Total . .	131	7·4	58,632	13·55
D. MISCELLANEOUS .	178	10·10	34,703	7·9

The principal causes of strikes were disputes over wages and hours : 82·5 per cent. of factories were affected by strikes of this kind, and 78·6 per cent. of the workers involved in them. Second in importance came strikes caused by the *personnel* of the administration. On an average, 45·4 per cent. of all strikes ended in favour of the employers, and only 28·2 per cent. in favour of the workers ; 21·8 per cent. ended in compromise ; the results of the remaining 4·6 per cent. were unrecorded.*

* *Ibid.*, pp. 227–228.

APPENDIX VI

THE RULES OF THE UNION OF WORKERS EMPLOYED IN THE TEA-DISTRIBUTING TRADE*

1. *Aim of the Union.* The aim of the union is the struggle for better economic and social conditions of workers, and the satisfaction of their spiritual needs.

(1) In order to fulfil this aim the union insists on the introduction of an eight-hour day and the payment of higher rates of wages ; the abolition of overtime and piece work ; the prohibition of the employment of children under sixteen years of age, and a six-hour working day for young persons under sixteen. Work must be stopped in every establishment for not less than forty-two hours at the week-end ; abolition of fines and deductions from wages ; free medical help, and payment of full wages during illness ; improvements of the sanitary conditions of the workshops ; introduction of State Insurance for old age, or incapacity for work ; the introduction of arbitration courts with equal representation of employers and workmen ; legal responsibility of employers for breaking existing factory laws ; the introduction of labour exchanges with the participation of workers in their management ; a fortnight's annual holiday with full pay.

(2) Introduction of factory inspectors elected by the workers themselves ; free judicial help for the workers ; the right to strike, freedom of meetings, organisations and press ; immunity of labour delegates ; official celebration of May 1st.

(3) Free education of children ; free access of workers to the public libraries ; the right of trade unions to open their own libraries, to hold concerts, public lectures, theatrical or cinema performances, etc.

2. *Funds of the Union.* The funds of the union consist of :—

(a) An entrance fee of 50 kopeks.

* " The History of One Union." Moscow, 1907, pp. 54–60.

(*b*) A monthly membership fee (3 per cent. of the monthly wage).

(*c*) Donations and contributions.

The funds of the union are divided into two parts : fixed and circulating capital. The expenditure of the fixed capital requires the consent of two-thirds of the total membership. The circulating capital may be spent : on benefits to strikers and their families ; on help to workers who have been victimised for their political views ; on the administration of the union and on the support of the labour press.

Note.—The union reserves the right to render financial assistance to strikers in other trades.

3. *Membership.* Every worker engaged in a tea-distributing firm is eligible for membership of the union, without consideration of sex, religion, political views, nationality, or age.

4. *Administration of the Union.* The union's office :—

(*a*) The general meetings of members.

(*b*) The Soviet of Delegates.

(*c*) The Executive Bureau.

(*d*) The Financial Commission.

(1) The soviet of delegates consists of delegates from each tea-distributing shop ; the workers in big firms send delegates from each shop, or department of the shop.

(2) The soviet of delegates elects a chairman, a secretary, an accountant and an executive bureau.

(3) Each delegate is responsible to the electors from whom he gets his instructions.

(4) The soviet of delegates is responsible to the union, and is obliged to issue monthly and annual reports.

(5) Any member of the soviet of delegates may be re-elected. For the election or re-election of the member to the soviet a majority of two-thirds of electors is required.

(6) The soviet of delegates meets not less than twice a month.

(7) Each shop has the right, provided half of its members agree, to call a special meeting of the soviet of delegates.

(8) The meeting of the soviet of delegates takes place provided four-fifths of its members are present.

Note.—The soviet of delegates has the right to invite to its meetings experts and specialists from outside. These persons have a consultative vote only.

(9) The general meeting of the union elects a financial commission for the monthly auditing of accounts and for the supervision of the activities of the soviet of delegates.

(10) A two-thirds majority of the members of the union is required for any additions or alterations to the existing rules of the union.

APPENDIX VII

THE DECLARATION TO THE BRITISH LABOUR DELEGATION OF THE RUSSIAN PRINTERS' UNION, PASSED AT A GENERAL MEETING OF THE UNION ON MAY 23RD, 1920

(EXTRACTS)

" WE welcome here the representatives of the British Labour Party and of the British Trades Union Congress, who have always shown brotherly sympathy towards us, Russian workers.

" The powerful working class of Great Britain raised its voice to stop the interference of foreign Imperialists in the internal affairs of Russia and in her right of self-determination. And now nobody dares to speak of intervention in Russian affairs. The proletariat of Great Britain has carried out its own intervention instead of that of the bourgeoisie.

" The attempt to isolate Russia economically and to stifle the Russian Revolution met with such resistance in the British Parliament that the blockade has been, at least formally, raised.

" We hope that the British working class will succeed in bringing about the complete abolition of the blockade and the re-establishment of economic relations between ourselves and Europe which we need so much.

" We hope also that the British working class will induce its Government to take the necessary steps to prevent the attempt of Poland to crush the Russian Revolution.

" The arrival of our British comrades in Russia will foster the international unity of the entire working class and will help to create a revolutionary Socialist International which will lead the working class of the world in the fight against Capitalism for the triumph of Socialism.

" All Russian Socialists are convinced that the triumph of Socialism in Russia is possible only if there is a Socialist revolution in the West. All endeavours to force Socialism upon one backward country alone will give no positive results. They will only lead to endless sufferings of the working population. That is why the Russian working class insists on the independent fight against its class enemies and on the independence of the labour organisations.

" Our present Government is not only a labour government : it is a labour-peasant government. The interests of workers and peasants are not always identical. The Russian working class must therefore be on its guard against any attempt of the present Government to go beyond necessary concessions to the peasantry and in any way to harm labour interests.

" Utopian endeavours, on the other hand, to enforce the immediate introduction of Socialism in Russia meet with desperate opposition from the peasantry ; they increase civil war and deepen the economic disorganisation of the country resulting from four years of civil war. The economic policy of the Soviet Government in introducing all-round nationalisation leads to a further disorganisation of the whole economic life of Russia.

" The National Economy of Russia cannot be improved by methods of violence against workers, by the militarisation of labour, by miserable rates of pay and long hours of work, etc. It can only be saved by the free and independent labour organisations. The heroic efforts of the working population will be crowned with success if the Government itself adopts a rational economic policy at home and abroad.

" A system of Reconstruction based on the compulsory labour of hungry and enslaved workers and on the destructive policy of the Government with its grotesque, parasitic administrative machine kept going out of the earnings of the working masses, will lead to further economic decay and the breakdown of the Revolution and of Socialism.

" This system of Reconstruction brings into opposition to the Government not only the peasantry but the workers themselves. The working class in Russia is decaying and losing its power and influence : it is dying out physically through hunger and illhealth : it is degenerating morally and politically, for the worker is on the one hand being converted into a bureaucrat in the factory, and on the other being subject to constant supervision exercised through the communist ' cells ' and commissars.

" The Communist Party has set itself up as the dictator

not only to the enemies of the working class, but to the working class itself. The Communist Party, which embraces only a small part of the working population and makes use of the state machinery and the country's resources, is imposing its will on the majority of the population and depriving the working masses of the right to have independent, free organisations.

" Freedom of the press and of election do not exist even for the workers themselves. The Communist Party alone may issue daily papers, journals, print pamphlets and books, giving no chance for the opposition to let itself be heard. All the socialist parties work ' underground,' in constant fear of being arrested, sent into exile or deprived of their right of citizenship. Many workers have been shot for their political views and for criticising the Communist Party, such as Goryatov, Krakovsky and others . . .

" There are only a few trade unions left whose Council or Præsidium has been properly elected ; and those trade unions whose officers have managed to keep in touch with the working masses are under constant watch and suspicion. The history of the Printers' Union over the last two years is the best confirmation of this.

" The Soviets in Russia represent only to a small extent the views of the workers and peasants. All non-Communist Soviets are usually dissolved. . . The Communist Party provokes risings and creates a counter-revolution among the working masses of the population.

" And in spite of all this we are against foreign intervention or the intervention of the old Russian bourgeoisie in our quarrel with the Communist Party. We admit only the intervention of the international proletariat in our affairs. We hope that the working class of other countries will bring moral pressure to bear on the Communist Party to give a chance to the Russian working class to fight for the economic regeneration of Russia, for their rights, for their liberation and for Socialism."*

* " Verbatim Report of the General Meeting of the Printers' Union." Moscow, 1920.

APPENDIX VIII

WAGES AND PRICES OF FOOD DURING THE YEARS 1901-15 *

WAGES in Russia, according to the investigation of Professor Manuilov, increased during the years 1901–09 by 18 per cent., prices of commodities by 37·6 per cent. The prices of some of the articles of consumption increased even more : rye bread, for instance, went up by 57 per cent., wheat bread by 66 per cent., rye flour by 72 per cent.

AVERAGE WAGES
(In roubles per year)

	1909	1910	1911	1912	1913
Moscow Province . .	228	243	241	248	253
Vladimir Province . .	188	186	192	190	188
Petersburg Province . .	342	355	365	375	384
Okrugs :					
Moscow . . .	202	209	213	216	219
Petersburg . . .	303	309	316	323	339
Warsaw	304	300	307	304	302
Kiev	176	179	191	191	197
Volga	206	204	216	221	232
Kharkov . . .	249	249	268	271	286
Average for the whole country	239	244	251	255	264

Professor Manuilov, comparing these data with the wages and food prices for 1909 and 1910, came to the following conclusions : " Owing to the rise in the cost of living and in house-rents, the average earnings of the Russian worker in

* This summary is based on the author's article on " Wages during the War," published in the " Materials as to the Rise of Prices during the War." University of Moscow, 1916, Vol. III., p. 211, etc.

1910 ought to have been at least between 232 and 237 roubles to cover food alone : and house-rents had also gone up considerably. If food and housing absorb half the earnings—house-rent having increased proportionately to food—we shall find that the average wage of 244 roubles a year, as quoted in the Reports of Factory Inspectors, gives no increase of the real wage compared with 1900–1901." *

The increase of wages in the main industrial Russian provinces and in some of the rayons (okrugs) for the years 1909–13 was given in the Reports of Factory Inspectors in the table on p. 196.

The increase of wages in 1911 and 1912 lagged behind the increase in prices. This may be seen from the following indices :—

PRICES

	1911	1912
Cereals	100	114
Animal produce . .	100	107
Average (all produce) .	100	106

WAGES

	1911	1912
Average wage of industrial workers for the whole country . . .	100	102

In the years 1913 and 1914 the changes in the average wages were as follows :—

WAGES OF FACTORY WORKERS IN THE MOSCOW PROVINCE

Branches of industry	In roubles		Indices	
	1913	1914	1913	1914
1. Cotton	219	223	100	102
2. Woollen	219	243	100	111
3. Silk	212	176	100	83
4. Flax, hemp . . .	138	172	100	125
5. Mixed textiles . .	261	231	100	89

* *Russkiya Viedomosti*, January 1st, 1912. A. Manuilov, "The Earnings of Russian Workers."

WAGES OF FACTORY WORKERS IN THE MOSCOW PROVINCE—*Continued*

Branches of industry	In roubles		Indices	
	1913	1914	1913	1914
6. Paper and graphic industry .	384	391	100	102
7. Woodworking . . .	347	367	100	106
8. Metal	409	403	100	99
9. Minerals	233	252	100	108
10. Animals	315	344	100	109
11. Food	253	241	100	95
12. Chemicals	277	287	100	104
13. Other	270	293	100	109
Average for the whole of industry	253	256	100	101

According to this table the average nominal wage went up by 1 per cent. The increase in wages in separate branches of industry was far from uniform. Moreover, a fall in wages took place in the silk, textile, metal and food industries. The maximum (25 per cent.) rise in wages occurred in Group 4—the flax and hemp industry—but that was due to the fact that only nine undertakings with 689 employees were engaged in this industry.

The prices of necessaries of life in the industrial centres of Russia for 1913–15 were as follows :—

	Prices for April (in kopeks)			Indices for April		
	1913	1914	1915	1913	1914	1915
Meat (second quality), per lb.	17	18	24	100	106	141
Rye bread (sour) . per pud	105	105	135	100	100	129
,, ,, (sweet) ,,	125	125	155	100	100	124
Buckwheat . ,,	150	168	328	100	112	219
Potatoes, 1 bushel . .	45	53	60	100	118	133
Sunflower oil . per pud	440	470	565	100	107	128
Tallow, melted . per lb.	25	25	28	100	100	112
Sauerkraut . per pud	90	90	95	100	100	106

The last two tables clearly indicate that the increase in wages lagged behind the increase in food prices : in other words, real wages went down. Indeed, while the average money wages for 1914 went up by 1 per cent., food prices rose approximately by 5 per cent. ; at the end of the same year by 15 per cent. to 20 per cent., and at the beginning of 1915 by 36 per cent.

At the beginning of 1915 food prices were rising rapidly and reached enormous heights for certain kinds of products. It is true that the mobilisation of industry in the summer of 1915 caused a great rise in wages of industrial workmen, though this rise continued to lag behind the rise in the cost of living.

BRIEF CHRONOLOGICAL TABLE

1613	The great *Zemsky Sobor* (Russian Parliament) elects the first Romanov Tsar.
1613–1645	The reign of Mikhail Fedorovich.
1645–1676	The reign of Alexey Mikhailovich.
1648–1649	The rebellion of Cossacks (Hetman Khmelnitsky).
1666	Trial of the Patriarch Nikon (*Raskol*, Old Believers).
1668–1671	The insurrection of Stepan Razin.
1682–1725	The reign of Peter the Great.
1700–1721	The great Northern War with Sweden.
1703	The foundation of St. Petersburg.
1721	Decree authorising factory owners to buy villages, together with their bondmen.
1725–1727	The reign of Catherine I.
1727–1730	The reign of Peter II.
1730–1740	The reign of Anne.
1736	Decree authorising factory owners to employ " freely-hired " labour (*Obrok* system).
1740–1741	The reign of Ivan VI.
1741–1743	The War with Sweden.
1741	The " Labour Regulation " and the " Workers' Rules."
1741–1761	The reign of Elizabeth (daughter of Peter the Great and Catherine I.).
1755	The foundation of the University of Moscow.
1756–1763	The Seven Years' War.
1750–1760	Riots and insurrections of peasants attached to factories (" possessional " workers).
1761–1762	The reign of Peter III.
1762–1796	The reign of Catherine II. (wife of Peter III.).
1773	The first partition of Poland.
1775	The abolition of independence of *Zaporozhie* (Ukrainian Cossacks).
1768–1774	The first Turkish War.

1773–1775	The insurrection of Pugachev.
1787–1791	The second Turkish War.
1788–1790	The War with Sweden.
1793–1795	The second and third partitions of Poland.
1796–1801	The reign of Paul I.
1801–1825	The reign of Alexander I.
1806–1812	Wars with Napoleon, Turkey and Sweden.
1812	The Fatherland War.
1821–1825	The rebellion of Decembrists.
1824	The " Third Department of His Majesty's Chancellery " (similar to the *G.P.U.* or *Cheka*) formed.
1825–1855	The reign of Nicholas I.
1830–1831	The insurrection of Poland.
1853–1856	The Crimean War.
1855–1881	The reign of Alexander II.
1861	The emancipation of serfs (February 19th).
1864	*Zemstvos* (Local Governments, Russian County Councils) formed.
1861–1870	The beginning of the Co-operative Movement in Russia.
1873–1875	*Narodnichestvo* (Movement to work among the people).
1874–1878	The South and North Russian Labour Unions (first political " underground " labour organisations) formed.
1879	The " *Narodnaya Volya* " (People's Will), the " *Zemlya i Volya* " (Land and Freedom) and the " *Cherny Perediel* " (Redistribution of the land) formed.
1881	Alexander II. killed.
1881–1894	The reign of Alexander III.
1883	The first Social-Democratic Organisation: " Emancipation of Labour Group " (G. Plekhanov, P. Axelrod, Vera Zassulich).
1885	The Morozov Strike.
1886	The " First Russian Labour Code."
1894–1917	The reign of Nicholas II.
1897	The $11\frac{1}{2}$ hours' working day. "Bund" (the Jewish Socialist Workers' Union) formed.

1898   The Russian Social Democratic Labour Party formed.

1900   The General Strike at Kharkov.

1901   The " *Zubatovshchina.*"

1903   Printers' strike in Moscow and the first " underground " Printers' Trade Union.

    Pogroms at Kishinev.

1904   The Japanese War.

    Gapon.

1905   January 9th.

    The Revolution.

    The Soviets of Workers' Delegates amongst the textile workers at Ivanovo-Voznessensk and amongst Printers in Moscow.—The beginning of legalised trade unionism.—The St. Petersburg and Moscow Soviets of Workers' Deputies.—Barricades in Moscow.

1906   The First Duma.

1912   The miners' strike in Lena Goldfields.

1915   The War.

1917   The Revolution.

    Abdication of Nicholas II. (March 15th).—The Provisional Government (Prince Lvov).—The First All-Russian Congress of Soviets (June–July).—Kerensky (July 21st).—Lenin, as Chairman of the Soviet Government (October).

1918   The Dissolution of the Constituent Assembly (January 19th).

    Brest-Litovsk Peace Treaty signed (March 3rd).

    Attempt on Lenin's life by Kaplan—a woman Social-Revolutionary—(August 30th).

1918–1921   The Civil War and the " War Communism."

1921–1926   The New Economic Policy (N.E.P.).

1922   The G.P.U. (the State Secret Political Department) formed.

    The Declaration of the establishment of the U.S.S.R.

1924   The death of Lenin (January 21st).

1928–1933   The First Five-Year Plan.

1933–1937   The Second Five-Year Plan.

BIBLIOGRAPHY

(The sources in languages other than Russian are marked with a *)

Afanassiev, A. " The National Wealth during the Reign of Peter the Great," " *Sovremennik,*" 1847.

Ainsaft, S. " The Trade-Union of Carpenters and Joiners." Moscow, 1928.

Antonov-Saratovsky, V. " The Proletarian Struggle." Moscow, Gosizdat, 1925.

Antoshkin, D. " A Short History of the Trade Union Movement in Russia." Moscow, 1928.

Archives of the History of Labour. 3 vols., Petrograd, 1921.

Arseniev, C. I. " A Statistical Survey of Russia." St. Petersburg, 1848. " Statistical Tables of the Russian State." 2 vols., St. Petersburg, 1818.

Balabanov, M. " Freedom of our Trade Unions." Moscow, 1906. " From 1905 to 1917." Moscow, Gosizdat, 1927.

*Baring, Maurice. " Half-a-minute Silence and Other Stories." New York, 1925.

Bazilevsky, B. " A Collection of Revolutionary Materials." St. Petersburg, 1905.

Bekhteyev, S. S. " Economic Progress of the last Forty-five Years." St. Petersburg, 1902.

Bieloussov, S. N. " A Collection of Articles on the History of the First Revolution of 1905." Moscow, Gosizdat, 1924.

Bogatur'ev, S. A. " An Experimental Table of the Russian Industry." Kazan, 1899. Edited by V. Burtsev, 1901–1907.

Bubnov, A. " The V.K.P.(b.) " (" The All-Union Communist Party of Bolsheviks.") Moscow, 1931.

Bulletins of the Museum of Labour Assistance of the Imperial Russian Technical Society. Moscow, 1905.

Bykov, A. N. " Factory Legislation and its Development in Russia." St. Petersburg, 1909.

" Century of Political Life in Russia." Edited by V. Burtsev and S. Stepniak. (S. M. Kravchinsky), London, 1897.

Chernyshevsky, N. "Works." Ed. 1862 and 1905.
" Consumers' Co-operation in the U.S.S.R." Moscow, Centrosoyus, 1935.
*" Co-operative Movement, The, in Soviet Russia." International Labour Office, Geneva, 1925.
" Decembrist Rising, The." Tsentrarkhiv, Moscow, 1925–29. 8 vols.
Declaration of the Printers' Trade Union (Verbatim Report). Moscow, 1920.
" Dekabristul : The Trial of the Decembrists." Edited by A. I. Hertsen. London, 1862.
Dmitriev, K. " Trade Unions in Moscow." 1907.
*Dobb, Maurice. " Soviet Russia and the World." London, 1932.
Dokukin, V. " Bolshevism and Menshevism in the Trade-Union Movement." Leningrad, Priboy, 1926.
Dubrovin, N. " Pugachev and his Associates." 3 vols., St. Petersburg, 1884.
Dzhanshiev, G. A. " The Epoch of the Great Reforms." Moscow, 1893.
Dzhivelegov, A. K. " Alexander I. and Napoleon." Moscow, 1915. " The War of the Fatherland." 2 vols., Moscow, 1912.
Elnitsky, A. " A History of the Labour Movement." Moscow, 1925.
Ezhov, V. (S. Zederbaum). " Peter Moisseyenko." Moscow, 1929.
Factory Inspectors' Reports (typewritten). Moscow, 1914.
Farforovsky, S. " Workers' Conditions in the Moscow Province." St. Petersburg, 1882. " The Life of Workmen in the Krenhelm Manufacturing Company's Works." In the *Archives*, Vol. II.
Finn-Enotayevsky, A. " The Contemporary Economic Conditions of Russia, 1890–1910." St. Petersburg, 1911.
First All-Russian Congress of Trade Unions. Verbatim Report. Moscow, 1918.
First Congress of the Supreme Economic Council. Verbatim Report. Moscow, 1918.
" First Russian Revolution, The : A Bibliography." (See : The Trade Union Movement.) The Communist Academy. Moscow, 1931.

Flerovsky, N. " The Conditions of the Working Class in Russia." St. Petersburg, 1869.

Fomin, P. I. " The Mining and Mineral Industry in Russia." Kharkov, 1915.

Georgievsky, P. I. " The Bibliography of the Russian Economic Literature." St. Petersburg, 1903.

Glinsky, B. B. " The History of the Russian Factories." In the " *Istorichesky Viestnik.*" St. Petersburg, 1898. Vol. V.

Gniedich, S. I. " The Life and Death of Stenka Razin." St. Petersburg, 1911.

Gorin, P. " A History of the Soviets of Workers' Deputies in 1905." Moscow, 1930.

Grinevich, D. " The Trade Union Movement in Russia." St. Petersburg, 1908 ; 2nd ed., 1922 ; 3rd ed., 1923.

Gurevich, L. " The People's Movement in St. Petersburg on the 9th January, 1905." In *Byloe*, 1906.

Hessen, J. " A History of Miners in U.S.S.R." 2 vols., Moscow, 1926. " The History of Peasants' Risings." In the *Archives of the History of Labour.* Vol. I., Petrograd, 1921.

" The History of One Trade Union." Edited by S. P. Turin. Moscow, 1907.

Il'in, V. (Lenin). " The Development of Capitalism in Russia." St. Petersburg, 1899, 1908.

*" Industries of Russia, The." Edited by Mendeleyev. The World Columbian Exposition, Chicago, 1893.

*International Labour Office. " Industrial Life in Soviet Russia, 1917–1923." Geneva, 1924.

Jahresbericht des Gewerkshaftskartells. Dresden, 1908.

Kanel, V. " Collective Agreements." Moscow, 1907.

Kantor, P. " Morosov Strike in 1885." In the *Archives of the History of Labour.* Vol. II.

Kargin, D. " Labour on the Nicholas Railway." In the *Archives of the History of Labour.* Vol. III.

Klyuchevsky, V. O. " A History of Russia." St. Petersburg, 1904, 1920, *London, 1926.

Kolokol (La Cloche). Geneva, Nos. 197–251.

Kolokolnikov, P. " The Trade Union Movement." Moscow, 1909, 1917.

Kolokolnikov, P., and Rapoport, S. " Trade Unions during 1905–1907." Moscow, 1925.

Kolpensky, V. " Strikes and Legislation Relating to Them."
In the *Archives of the History of Labour.* Vol. II.

Koltsov, D. " The Russian Labour Movement." In the
Liberation Movement. Vols. I. and II.

Korfut, M. " The Insurance Act of 1912." In the *Red
Chronicle*, 1928, No. 1/25.

Kosminykh-Lanin, S. M. " Boarding Artels." Moscow,
1915.

Kovalevsky, M. " Economic Structure of Russia." St.
Petersburg, 1899.

*Kropotkin, P. A. " Letters to S. P. Turin, 1917–1920." *Le
Monde Slave*, Paris, January, 1925.

Kulibin, S. " The Mining Industry in Russia." St. Petersburg, 1886.

*Kulisher, J. M. *Russiche Wirtschaftsgeschichte.* Jena, 1925.

" Labour in the U.S.S.R." Moscow, Gosizdat, 1932.

Labour. A Journal. St. Petersburg, 1906–1908.

" Labour Movement during the War." Edited by M. G.
Fleer. Tsentrarkhiv, Moscow, 1925.

" Labour Movement in 1917." *Archives of the October Revolution*, 1926.

" Labour Movement in 1917." Edited by B. L. Meller and
A. M. Pancratova. Moscow, Tsentarchiv, 1926.

Labour Thought. A Journal. 1899.

*Labry, R. " L'Industrie Russe et la Révolution." Paris,
1919.

Lappo-Danilevsky, A. " The Russian Industrial Companies
in the First Half of the Eighteenth Century." St.
Petersburg, 1899.

Law Codes of the Russian Empire : 1818, 1857, 1913. St.
Petersburg.

" Liberation (The) Movement in Russia." 4 vols., St.
Petersburg, 1909.

Litvinov-Falinsky, V. " Factory Legislation." St. Petersburg, 1900.

*Lloyd, C. M. " Trade Unionism." London. Ed. 1928.

Lyadov, M. N. " A History of the Russian Social-Democratic
Party." Moscow, 1906.

**Manchester Guardian* (The)*. January, 1905.

Manolov, I. I. " Essay on the Contemporary Trade and
Industrial Development of the Russian Empire." St.
Petersburg, 1899.

Manuilov, A. " The Earnings of the Russian Worker." In the *Russkiya Viedomosti*. Moscow, 1912, January 1st.
*Marchal, Charles. " Le Socialisme en Russie." Paris, 1860.
Martov, L. " The Development of the Labour Movement." In *The Liberation Movement*.
Martov, L. " A History of Russian Social Democracy, 1898–1907." Moscow, 1923.
" Materials on the Labour Question." Stuttgart, 1903.
" Materials Relating to the Economic Conditions of Metal Workers." St. Petersburg, 1909.
" Materials Relating to the Regeneration of Russia." 8 vols. 1874–81.
*Mavor, James. " An Economic History of Russia." London, 1914. " The Russian Revolution." London, 1928.
Metalworkers' News. A Journal. Nos. 1–3. 1917–18.
Migulin, P. P. " The Regeneration of Russia : Economic Essays." Kharkov, 1910.
Mikulin, A. A. " The Factory Inspectors in Russia, 1882–1906." Kiev, 1906.
*Milyukov, P. " Russia and its Crisis." London, 1905.
Monossov, S. " A History of the Revolutionary Movement, 1789–1871." Kharkov, 1925.
" Narodnoye Khosyaistvo of the U.S.S.R." Moscow, 1924.
Nekrasov, N. " Poems." St. Petersburg, 1919.
Nevsky, V. " The Lena Goldfields." In the *Krassnaya Letopis*, 1922, Nos. 2–3.
Nikitin, A. " The Truth about Events in the Lena Goldfields." Moscow, 1924.
" ' Nineteen Five ' in St. Petersburg." Moscow, 1925.
Nisselovich, A. " History of Factory Legislation in the Russian Empire."
Orlovsky, P. " The Duma and the Labour Question." St. Petersburg, 1906.
Ovsyannikov, N. N. " Decembrist Rising The." Moscow, 1920. " On the Eve of the Labour Movement." Moscow, 1919.
Ozerov, I. Kh. " Economics of Russia and her Financial Policy." Moscow, 1905. " The Life of Labour." Moscow, 1904. " The Labour Question in Russia." Moscow, 1906.

*Pares, Sir Bernard. "A History of Russia." London, 1926, 1935.

"Past and Present of Trade Unions in Russia." Edited by J. Milonov, Moscow, 1927.

Pazhitnov, K. "Hours of Work in the Mining Industry." In the *Archives of the History of Labour.* Vols. II. and III. "Labour Conditions in Russia." St. Petersburg, 1906. "Strikes and Riots of Factory Workers." In the *Archives.* Vols. I. and II.

Pecheta, V. T., and Others. "The National War, 1812–1912." Moscow, 1911.

Piantkovsky. S. "Zubatovshchina." In the *Krasny Archiv,* Moscow, 1922.

*Platonov, S. Th. "History of Russia." St. Petersburg, 1901, 1910. (In English : London, 1925.)

Plekhanov, G. "History of the Russian Social Thought." Moscow, 1914. "N. G. Chernyshevsky." St. Petersburg, 1910. "Revolutionary Movement in Russia." Moscow, 1919. "Two Years at Home." Paris, 2 vols.

Pod'yachev, S. "Among Workers." St. Petersburg, 1905. "Works." Leningrad, 1927.

Pogozhev, A. "Statistics of Industrial Workers in Russia." St. Petersburg, 1906.

Pokrovsky, M. "History of the Revolutionary Movement." 2 vols. Moscow, 1926. "Russian History." Moscow, 1910 ; Leningrad, 1924. *"A Russian History." London, 1930. *"Brief History of Russia." London, 1933.

Polyansky, N. "Strikes among Workers and the Criminal Code." 1907.

*Popov, N. "Consumers' Co-operatives in the U.S.S.R." London, 1927.

Printers' Union General Meeting (The), Verbatim Report. Moscow, 1920.

Prokopovich, S. "Co-operative Movement." Moscow, 1913. "Uber die Bedingungen der Industriellen Entwicklun Russlands."* In the *Archive für Sozialwissenschaft.* Ergänzungheft 10, 1913. "Workers' Budgets in St. Petersburg, 1909."

Proletarian. A Journal. 1906–1909.

Proletarian Revolution. A Journal. Moscow, Gosizdat, 1921–32.

*" Protokoll der Verhandlungen des dritten Kongresses der Gewerkschaften." Frankfurt a/Maine, 1899.

Pumpyansky, L. " Industrial Labour." In the *Economist*. Petrograd, 1922. No. 1.

Radin, B. " The First Soviet of Workers' Deputies." St. Petersburg, 1906.

Red Chronicle (The). A Journal. Moscow, Gosizdat, 1922–32.

" Report of the Russian Ministry of the Interior." Paris, 1909.

" Results of an Economic Survey of Russia." Moscow, 1892.

*Rhodes, Cicely. " A History of the Trades Council, 1860–1875." London, 1920.

Rozhkov, N. A. " Historical Essays." Moscow, 1906. " History of Russia." Petrograd, 1923. " Town and Village in Russian History." Moscow, 1904.

" Russia at the End of the Nineteenth Century." Edited by V. I. Kovalevsky.

" Russian Law and the Worker." Stuttgart, 1902.

Semevsky, V. I. " The Peasants during the Reign of Catherine II." 2 vols. St. Petersburg, 1903. " Workers in the Siberian Goldfields." St. Petersburg, 1898.

Social Democrat, The. A Journal. Geneva, 1904, 1905.

Solov'yev, E. A. " Working People and the New Ideas." St. Petersburg, 1906.

Solov'yev, S. M. " History of Russia." St. Petersburg, 1911. " Public Lectures on Peter the Great." St. Petersburg, 1903.

Somov, S. " History of the Social-Democratic Party." In *Byloe*, 1907, No. 4/16.

" South Russian Labour Unions." Edited by V. V. Maksakov and V. I. Nevsky. Tsentrarkhiv, Moscow, 1924.

" Soviet of Workers' Deputies (Lawsuit)." St. Petersburg, 1907.

" *Sovremennik.*" A Journal. 1847–66.

Spassky, P. K. " History of Trade and Industry." St. Petersburg, 1910.

Statistical Review (The). Moscow, 1927, 1928.

Stopany, A. M. " Workers' Budgets in the Oilfields." Baku, 1916.

Storch, H. F. " Historisch-Statistisches Gemälde des Russischen Reichs." Riga, Leipzig, 1797–1802 ; in French, " Tableau Historique et statistique de l'Empire de Russie à la fin du XVIII. siècle." Paris, 1801. " Russland unter Alexander I." St. Petersburg, 1804.

Struve, P. B. " A Characteristic of Russian Factory Legislation." St. Petersburg, 1902. " Past and Present of Russian Economics."* Cambridge, 1917. " The Law of 2nd, June, 1897." In the *Narodnoye Khozyaistvo*, March, 1902. St. Petersburg.

" Survey of the Chief Branches of the Manufacturing Industry in Russia." St. Petersburg, 1845.

Svyatlovsky, V. V. " The Trade Union Movement." St. Petersburg, 1907 ; Moscow, 1925.

*Tawney, R. H. " The Agrarian Problem in the Sixteenth Century." London. Ed. 1912.

" Trade Unions' Second Conference." Verbatim Report. St. Petersburg, 1906.

*" Trade Union Movement (The) in Soviet Russia." Geneva, 1927.

*" Trade Unions' British Delegation to Russia." The Official Report. London, 1925.

*Trotsky, L. " The History of the Russian Revolution." 3 vols. London, 1934.

Tugan-Baranovsky, M. " The Russian Factory in the Past and Present." St. Petersburg, 1898 ; Moscow, 1922.

Turin, S. P. " Labour and Wages during the War." In the *Investigation into the Rise of Prices*. Moscow, 1915. Vol. III. " Moscow Trades Council." Moscow, 1913. " Workers' Family Budgets in U.S.S.R."* In the *International Labour Review*. Geneva, 1929. Vol. 20.

Vanag, N., and Tomsinsky, S. " Economic Development of Russia." Moscow, Gosizdat, 1928.

Vladimirov, V. " The Events in the Lena." Moscow, Gosizdat, 1932.

Voice of Labour. A Journal. Kiev, 1913.

Voice of the Social Democrat. A Journal. Geneva, 1909, 1910.

Voznessensky, S. " The Economic Development and Class War in Russia." Petrograd, 1924.

" *Vpered.*" A Journal. Geneva, 1905.

*Webb, Sidney and Beatrice. " History of Trade Unionism."
London. Ed. 1919.

Yanzhul, I. " Labour Conditions in the Moscow Province."
St. Petersburg, 1884. " Reminiscences of a Factory
Inspector." St. Petersburg, 1907.

GLOSSARY

Artel . . .	" An association formed to carry out specified units of work, or to carry on certain industries, or to render personal services on the joint responsibility of the members of the *artel* and for their joint account."
Bolshevik . .	Member of the left wing of the Social-Democratic Party.
Bolshinstvo . .	Majority.
Boyar . . .	" Free follower of a prince ; member of highest social and political class in Russia until Peter the Great established the ' Table of Ranks ' (1722), which made rank technically dependent on service position."
Byloe . . .	Past.
Centrosoyus . .	Central Union.
Cherny . . .	Black.
Cherny Perediel .	Redistribution of the land.
Duma . . .	Assembly, the Russian Parliament.
Ispravnik . .	Captain of the Police.
Izvozchik . .	Cab-driver.
Knut . . .	Whip.
Komsomol . .	The Union of the Communist Youth.
Kooperatsia . .	Co-operative Society.
Krasny Arkhiv .	Red Archives.
Kvass . . .	Home-made cider.
Menshevik . .	Member of the right wing of the Social-Democratic Party.
Menshinstvo . .	Minority.
Mir . . .	Village local administration.
Moskovskiya Viedomosti . .	The Moscow News.
Narod . . .	People.
Narodnaya Volya .	The People's Will.

Narodnichestvo	.	A movement of the Russian intelligentsia to help the people.
Nashe Dielo .	.	Our Affairs.
Obrok . .	.	Money tax.
Okhrana .	.	A Department of the Secret Police.
Osvobozhdenie Truda .	.	The Emancipation of Labour.
Podstrekatel .	.	Initiator of a riot.
Pogromschiki	.	Organisers of a pogrom.
Possessionye Krestiane.		Peasants attached to the State or private factories.
Proletarskaya Revolutsia .	.	The Proletarian Revolution.
Pud . .	.	36·11 lbs.
Rabochy Soyus	.	The Workers' Union.
Russkiya Viedomosti		*The Russian News.*
Soviet . .	.	Council.
Stanichnaya Isba	.	District (Cossacks) Peasants' Court.
Starosta	.	Elder, headman, foreman, steward, monitor.
Starshina	.	Elder, headman.
Trud . .	.	Labour.
Trudovaya Groupa	.	Labour Group.
Versta . .	.	·66 English mile.
Votchinye Krestiane		Peasants who were obliged to work in the hereditary estates or undertakings of noblemen.
Vpered . .	.	Forward.
Yassnaya Polyana	.	Leo Tolstoy's estate
Zachinshchik .	.	Instigator.
Zastava. .	.	Border of a suburb.
Zemsky Sobor	.	Russian Parliament.
Zemskaya Mirskaya Izba .	.	Local peasants' Court.
Zemstvo	.	Local Government.
Zubatovshchina	.	" Police Socialism in Russia," originated by Zubatov.

INDEX OF SUBJECTS

INDEX OF PERSONS

OTHER PUBLICATIONS OF THE AUTHOR

In English

" Russian Local Government during the War and the
Union of Zemstvos." In collaboration with Prince
V. A. Obolensky and T. I. Polner.
Carnegie Endowment for International Peace. New Haven,
Yale University Press. 1930. pp. xii. + 317.

Articles

In the *Slavonic and East European Review*. London :
" Nicholas Chernyshevsky and John Stuart Mill "
(Vol. IX., 1930).
" The Foreign Trade of the U.S.S.R." (Vol. X., 1931).
" The Second Five-Year Plan " (Vol. XI., 1932).
" A Bibliography of Russian Publications " (Vol. X.,
1932).
In the *Encyclopædia of the Social Sciences*, New York, 1933.
Vol. X. :
" A. A. Manuilov."
In the *International Labour Review*, Geneva :
" Workers' Family Budget Enquiries in Soviet Russia "
(reprinted in the present book).

In Russian

" The Moscow Trades Council." Moscow, 1913, pp. xv. +
192.
" The Labour Problem in England." London, 1920, pp. 80.
" All-Russian Unions of Zemstvos and Towns in England."
London, 1921, pp. 46.

Articles

In the *History of One Union*, Moscow, 1907 :
" The Soviets of Delegates."
In the *Help Worker*, Moscow, 1907 :
" The Consumers' Co-operative Societies."

OTHER PUBLICATIONS

In the *Materials as to the Rise of Prices during the War*, published by the University of Moscow in 1915. Vol. III. :
" Wages in Russia during the War."

In the *Care of the Population in England*. A Collection of Articles with a Foreword by S. P. Turin, and an Introduction by Sir Paul Vinogradov. London, 1920 :
" Child Labour in England."

In the *Annales Contemporaines*. Paris, 1920. Vol. I. :
" Guild Socialism."